WITTENBERG MEETS THE WORLD

Wittenberg Meets the World

*Reimagining the Reformation
at the Margins*

Alberto L. García *&* John A. Nunes

WILLIAM B. EERDMANS PUBLISHING COMPANY
GRAND RAPIDS, MICHIGAN

Wm. B. Eerdmans Publishing Co.
2140 Oak Industrial Drive NE, Grand Rapids, Michigan 49505
www.eerdmans.com

ISBN 978-0-8028-7328-6

Library of Congress Cataloging-in-Publication Data

A catalog record for this book is available from the Library of Congress

To the people of God in the diaspora,
who sing, suffer, struggle, and hope in the language of our ancestors
with the fervor of our grandparents,
the faith and trust of Martin Luther King Jr. and Oscar Romero,
the boldness and resolution of Rosa Parks and the undocumented
Latino students in the United States,
the vision of Virgilio Elizondo and Gudina Tumsa,
and the wisdom of our parents.

And to our families:
To Mori, my wife and best friend, to the memory of my mother
Norma and father Antonio, my children Yvette and Phil, and my
loving granddaughter Alana, entrusted with the hope of a new
day.—ALG

To Monique, whose thoughtfulness puts flesh on my bones
(Sirach 26:13), to my six children, and to my expanding entourage of
grandchildren.—JAN

Contents

Foreword

"Reimagining" is what authors Alberto García and John Nunes are doing, and they make no secret of hoping that readers will join them in doing so. Before "reimagining" anything, we find ourselves "imagining" in the first place. Their subject is the Reformation, in this case the Lutheran Reformation and its offspring and parallels. Readers of this book live in a world where seventy million people of faith are called "Lutheran." Imagine them, or some of them: will a reader picture the typical Lutheran as, say, a Pennsylvanian or a Minnesotan or, beyond North American shores, a Norwegian or a German? In another context, popular-cultural terms, imagine a culture modeled by retired radio host Garrison Keillor as he dealt with a bachelor farmer living in a town called Lake Wobegon. Will that image do for "typical" Lutheranism?

No. García and Nunes make clear that they do not want readers to settle for stereotypes. They announce that they want to engage in disruption, but not of a kind that produces chaos. Instead, it is *creative* disruption, upheavals that are designed to startle and awaken otherwise contented, routine, and apathetic believers. The authors consistently delight in disrupting whatever is considered typical and "settled." They talk much about the goal of experiencing the gospel "in the margins" and listening to, learning from, and serving with believers "on the margins." Consistently they want readers to rethink their positions in society and culture and listen to the Sermon on the Mount, the Gospels, the words of Scripture, and preaching from fresh angles. They hope that Lutherans and non-Lutherans who want to understand them, their faith, and their churches will listen.

Are we readers ready to face disruption, to be jostled? We had better be because these chapters are designed to unsettle readers so they can thereupon be quickened. Think of this: Lutheran followers of their act of reimagining are henceforth more likely to picture the Lutheran individual as a black Ethiopian rather than a white American, a Tanzanian rather than a Wisconsonian, an Indonesian rather than an Indianan. Outrageous, is it, to be called to reimagine along such lines? It is not, if one wants to acquire an accurate picture of living Lutherans. There are more Lutherans in Ethiopia (6.3 million), Tanzania (5.8 million), and Indonesia (5.8 million) than in any other nation except Germany and Sweden. Whoever has studied the religious practices in the latter two nations will there find diminishing churchly populations that, with some grand exceptions, also manifest dwindling piety and worship—the opposite of what is happening among millions of Lutherans in the Southern world. By the way, eighth among the nations in the church numbers game is the United States, with four million Lutherans.

With the location of a people comes a style, a set of ways of doing things, including in their gathering for the Word and sacrament. In general, the Lutheranism of most imaginings by people in the Euro-American world can be described as being "septentrionalist," a word that readers are permitted to dispose of, once the point of recalling it has passed. "Septentrionalism" is a word seldom used now, but it was and is fashionable, for example, among lovers of southern European Renaissance art, which in their eyes outshone the quieter, colder northern European Renaissance art. Think of it simply as "northernism," which is what the first centuries of the Lutheran Reformation embodied and expressed.

Let me hasten to add that García and Nunes are not dismissing the Luther of the North—he was, after all, wholly of the North. He seldom "imagined" the work of the church reached farther than Saxony and its environs. He came back from his one foray south into Rome as quickly as he could. The authors are not by any means rejecting the Lutheranism of the North with its catechisms, its Johann Sebastian Bach, its great inherited hymnody and thousands of faithful congregations. The two authors may criticize much of what does go on in Lutheran churches, for example, of Old World Germany and New World Canada. But they mainly provide tools for constructive criticism to be used for "reimagining" Lutherans and their activities and productions everywhere, beginning at home, wherever that may be. Let me stress this, which readers will soon discover on their own: García and Nunes concentrate on the main affirmations and doctrinal insights of classical world Lutheranism. They are far too "at home" as Lutherans to let anyone, including themselves, off the hook in their analysis. Take a key sample: all humans of faith are *simul justus et peccator*, that is, they are "at the same time" "justified" and "sinners." But such believers are all called to lives of repentance, the change of heart effected by the Holy Spirit and made possible by the love and action of Christ.

If all believers are definably, by nature and situation, "in the same boat," then why throw out lifeboats by accenting not what they have in common, culturally and universally, but their particulars, depending on their locations, cultures, and experiences? Here's why: having just tested readers' patience with one barbaric term, "septentrionalism," we'll now slip in another difficult-sounding term that can be of great help to reimaginers. That word is "hermeneutics," a word favored by scholars who ponder texts, considering what they do and what they mean and how they mean. These scholars recognize what everyone can recognize if they are called to do so: that every person or group of persons has an angle of vision, born of their location, heritage, talents, and experiences. Does the García-Nunes duo imply or even contend that *everyone* has a viewpoint, whether in writing or interpreting or broadcasting a text, and that realizing this can be an aid to understanding and action? Emphatically "Yes."

For example, we regularly listen to accounts of how different Gospel texts sound to people of prosperity on the one hand and to those of want on the other. Or think how different ministry is among believers who have suffered sexual abuse versus ministry that serves those who have been surrounded through the years with freedom and nurturing care. Good preachers, confessors, consolers, and inspirers all know better than to minister in a "one-size-fits-all" mode, even if they serve with one gospel in one church. The messages and actions of believers in congregations located in affluent suburbs are likely to respond to Christian appeals differently from those who exist in utter poverty.

I was drawn to this book, and I hope many others will be. I also hope that, with the disruptions it promotes, will come knowledge and motivation for us to re-examine our place in respect to those who are or are often considered to be "on the margins." Are we ready for creative disruption? How do we find ourselves when we meet the "others"? Luther taught us to get perspective on ourselves. For instance, I grew up in small towns on the Great Plains in the 1930s, when the big D-words like Depression, Drought, Dust Bowl, Disappointment, and Despair shadowed what our fellow believers all around us were going through. We had to learn about the gospel among "others" and among our own, as change came. Where are we now? García and Nunes, by telling some stories of "elsewhere," help readers find themselves "here," where we are called to "eco-justice" and to care for others whom we have overlooked before. The new vision is liberating.

Let me cite one more characteristic disruption of convention that is perpetrated by creative agitators García and Nunes. It has to do less with the map, and its North or South, East or West, than it does with the positions and experiences of human persons and, in this case again, with individual persons in isolation or persons-in-community or society. Those who serve people in these great varieties will introduce and work with the concept of direction, as in power or influence "from below," as opposed to "from above." García and Nunes, when paying attention to influences and needs "from below," are not against order. They recognize its value, but they do question why all the impulses, initiatives, monitoring, suggesting, and energizing in the church has to come from the powerful, from hierarchy, as it were. The gospel of Christ, the Lutheran witness to the priesthood of all believers, and the common experience of baptism are very much on their minds, and they hope these will be ever more so among others after they have read this book. While readers can get practical advice in general about living in the light of the Reformation, the authors have specifically urged and exemplified a basic approach: we are to *listen*, listen to the Word and to those who respond to it, and then not simply hold to or impose our own customs, ways, and language. No, they and we all are to be humble and graced from God above so we can all respond to those who respond "from below," a company of believers to which all of us can listen and which we are freshly enabled to "imagine" joining.

MARTIN E. MARTY
Fairfax M. Cone Distinguished Service Professor Emeritus
The University of Chicago

Preface

We, the authors, are evangelical catholic theologians and pastors. As such, our theological work is centered in the gospel of Jesus Christ and in the catholic tradition of the church, which is ecumenical in nature by seeking the unity of the church. We are also children of the diaspora, shaped and formed by our families and communities of faith at the margins. This collaborative work bears this vision and imprint. We ask, in true Lutheran fashion, as a way of reflection and collaboration (*teología en conjunto*): what does it mean to reimagine the Reformation from the margins?

Our work of reimagining is unique in that it is dually situated: we are both rooted deliberatively in a Lutheran tradition, on the one hand, and in postcolonial critique, on the other. This pertains to our focus on the locus of justification—understood by Lutherans as the doctrine on which the church stands or falls. Ensuing from this core principle are three loci, ways in which many confessional churches organize themselves for ministry: within the operative categories of *martyria* (witness), *diakonia* (service), and *koinōnia* (witness). These marks of the church are widely agreed on in the evangelical catholic tradition as correlatives. Using these permits an intercultural conversation—which ordinarily might be difficult for theologians writing from the perspective of the margins using a postcolonial critique.

Preface

We use the term "postcolonialism" to describe a method concerned theologically with dilemmas of existence among communities formerly under colonial regimes. This impacts themes related to sociocultural identity, personal meaning amid severe deprivation, and a community's posture vis-à-vis eternal things and the problem of evil, theodicy. While we are not focused on the victimhood often emerging from legacies of suffering, we are profoundly aware of the history of oppression that, at times, was promoted and promulgated by ecclesial structures. As such, we must beware of contemporary neo-colonializing consequences of well-intended church relations. As Renu Juneja aptly summarizes: "Colonizers not only colonize the history of the colonized but subjugate their imaginations as well."[1] In creative resistance to this, we engage in this work of reimagination. We realize, therefore, the challenges to our task.

Imagination is the embryo of either anxiety or creativity. Anxiety forecloses the possibility of empathy—such anxiety is often exacerbated by xenophobia or the loss of privilege in the midst of increasing multiethnic pluralism. Imagination can give birth to creativity that, when cultivated, can enhance the way Christians relate to one another and to the world. Hence, we opt for the intensive prefix "re-." In the same way that the Reformation recaptured the church's gospel emphases, so to *reimagine* implies both a reconsideration of the implications of the Reformation and a creative revisiting of this tradition for the twenty-first century. This involves a bold incarnational point of departure. It involves the affirmation of *solus Christus* (Christ alone) from below. It involves, therefore, a close listening to the people as we creatively revisit our tradition from this time and place. This listening, we believe, is congruent to a postcolonial theologizing.

A key component of our postcolonial theologizing is that we are suspicious of the use of correct and proper theological premises

---

1. Renu Juneja, *Caribbean Transactions: The Making of West Indian Culture in Literature* (London: Macmillan, 1996), iii.

for the sake of enslaving the strange communities of faith with idolatries of power. We have learned through our theological inquiries from the margins that Luther was also suspicious of the use of theological premises and reason when they were employed to enslave people of faith. Postcolonial thinking wakes us from our slumbers of theological and rational idolatrous certainty. This does not mean that we are relativists in terms of theological constructions. What it means is that our starting point for doing theology is our historical borderland location. It is not by our thinking that we become genuine Christian theologians. We are who we are, as Walter Mignolo so aptly describes, because we dwell in the borderlands and have been marked by the colonial wound.[2] Postcolonial thinking subverts the Cartesian dictum, "I think, therefore I am." Postcolonial thinking affirms first and foremost "I am where I think." Our universal thinking begins with this particular "I am." We are also cognizant that our communities of faith understand this "I am" as communal. There is no identity or theologizing apart from our communities of faith. This identity is marked and shaped by a life under the cross. In the words of Luther: "For one becomes a theologian by living, by dying, by being damned: not by mere intellectualizing, reading and speculating."[3] This life at the borderlands involves a certain risk and vulnerability because we are forced to hear other voices in their contexts and need, rather than listen only to our theological clichés or the sounds of our human righteousness.

This book attempts, therefore, to join the work of those addressing a lacuna in five-hundredth-anniversary Reformed scholarship. Some of the fastest growth numerically among Lutherans and other Christian traditions—especially Pentecostals and Catholics—has been in the so-called developing world. These communities (African, African American, Latin American, and Asian) have been tra-

---

2. Walter D. Mignolo, *Global Histories/Local Designs: Coloniality, Subaltern Knowledges, and Border Thinking* (Princeton: Princeton University Press, 2012), xiv.

3. Translated by Alberto García from Luther's *Operationes in Psalmos* (1519–21) (*WA* 5:163).

ditionally underdeveloped and under-considered within the realms of systematic and historical theology as they relate to their contexts. There has been, to borrow a term, a "failure of imagination." We must continue, therefore, the process of reforming the church. We must continue to do this through a process of reimagination. Otherwise we become complacent to the created tragedies of our times. Our histories of suffering have been neglected or silenced by mainstream theologians. Our hopes and dreams of grace have been stifled by the proclamation of a disembodied gospel. But we are hopeful.

We are hopeful because our collaborative work is an exercise in the Spirit and of the imagination. We find a similar dynamics in the Acts of the Apostles. We call on the living God, the Holy Spirit of Pentecost, to guide our way and renew our imagination. Our renewed imagination by the urging of the Spirit permits empathy to flourish in our theological and pastoral work. It permits us to experience something we have either never experienced or something we are currently ourselves incapable of experiencing; so, we can "rejoice with those who rejoice, weep with those who weep" (Rom. 12:15), as we accompany others through life's pilgrimage in spite of the non-resemblance of our experiences. This is how we walk at this opportune time in our commemoration of the Reformation five hundred years later (1517–2017). Our hope is, therefore, that this collaborative work not be taken as one more attempt to live in the glories of the past. Our tradition, our moorings, is important. But Christ alone, the *solus Christus*, incarnationally present at this time and place, is our guiding light. We pray that this work will prove useful and salutary for those who wish to minister at the margins in the twenty-first century in North America.

We, the authors, have spent several years sharing our questions and dreams born out of our diaspora experiences and evangelical catholic faith. In reading the chapters that follow—1, 3, 5, and 7 written by Alberto and 2, 4, 6, and 8 written by John—readers will recognize why we have joined to lift our voices together to give a witness to our Christian faith. Readers should consider this work as a pilgrimage of faith. It is not done yet. It will be continued, for this is the work of pilgrims, calling others to join us as pilgrims in the reimagination and renewal of our witness to church and world.

We would like to thank Martin E. Marty, Melanie Trexler, Justo L. González, and Carl E. Braaten for their encouragement and insights in the writing of this book. There is also a myriad of other scholars and theologians that we would like to thank in the writing of this book. How they inspired our work will be duly noted throughout this book.

Abbreviations

BC	*The Book of Concord*
EECMY	Ethiopian Evangelical Church Mekane Yesus
ELCA	Evangelical Lutheran Church of America
ESV	English Standard Version
FC	*Formula of Concord*
FCTC	*From Conflict to Communion: Lutheran-Catholic Common Commemoration of the Reformation*
LCMS	Lutheran Church–Missouri Synod
LW	*Luther's Works*
LWF	Lutheran World Federation
NIV	New International Version
NRSV	New Revised Standard Version
RV	La Santa Biblia, Reina Valera
WA	*D. Martin Luthers Werke: Kritische Gesamtausgabe, Schriften*

CHAPTER 1

God of Justification, God of Life

A Borderland Reimagining of the Reformation

My heart is restless! Today we live in a world and society that is in a bitter struggle *mano a mano*. This is more evident to us today because of modern technology. Many grave images of violence and death impact and disturb us instantly as everyday occurrences. They have become as saturated in our lives as the air that we breathe. Death is not just a distant neighbor present in Africa, the Middle East, and Latin America. Death is not just a global malady. Death surrounds us in the communities in which we live and work in the United States. Its stench drowns in many ways the fragrant scent of blooming flowers in the spring.

The restlessness of my heart is not only due, however, to the presence of a culture of death in our world. It impacts my Christian faith as I find ways of giving witness to the living God in light of the sign of the times. This same restlessness has become apparent to me in the narratives of many communities of faith at the end of the twentieth and the beginning of the twenty-first centuries. Victor and Irene Chero expressed this in a poignant and forceful manner as they spoke on behalf of the shanty towns of Lima, Peru, before Pope John Paul II in 1985. They gave witness to the premature deaths that their community was experiencing and the uncertain future that their families were facing because of the total disregard for life present before them. But they also expressed "with renewed force, a profession of faith: 'we believe in the God of life.'"[1] Gustavo Gutiérrez describes this to be the faith of emigrants as "they are driven by their understanding of God and their desire for a different kind of life."[2] This valiant quest by the Cheros and their community of faith was summarized with this poignant witness from them: "We struggle for life in the midst of death."[3] As these emigrants, as well as other Latin American and Caribbean emigrants, have become immigrants in the United States, their restless hearts continue to search for the living God in the midst of their perilous situations.

The search for the God of life is a universal struggle and reality in our present world. It is, in effect, the burning issue and quest of perceptive and sensitive theologians and of people of faith in our present *kairos*. Elizabeth Johnson captures this quest for the living God in today's world in *Quest for the Living God: Mapping Frontiers in the Theology of God*.[4] This quest is not an academic or intellectual exercise but rather a journey with people in their everyday lives as they question and search for the living God in our present world. US Latino and Latina theologians call this quest living *en lo cotidiano*. Jeanette Rodriguez, a US Latina theologian, clearly affirms the necessity of this quest and theological reformulation for our times: "Both African and Latin American theologians explain that their way to a theological reformulation is firmly and deeply planted in human life, where they believe the Holy Spirit lives and acts."[5]

This quest requires, therefore, that all Christian churches be in a state of reformation as they seek to bear witness to the living

1. Gustavo Gutiérrez, *The God of Life*, trans. Matthew J. O'Connell (Maryknoll, NY: Orbis, 1991), xi.

2. Gutiérrez, *The God of Life*, xi.

3. Gutiérrez, *The God of Life*, xi.

4. Elizabeth A. Johnson, *Quest for the Living God: Mapping Frontiers in the Theology of God* (New York: Continuum, 2011), 1–4.

5. Jeanette Rodriguez, *Stories We Live (Cuentos Que Vivimos): Hispanic Women's Spirituality* (New York: Paulist, 1996), 2.

God in our present time. The word "reformation" does not mean abandonment of our foundation or our past. The Scriptures and our creedal foundations as well as our Christian traditions are crucial to this quest. However, it also requires reimagination. The reimagining of the gospel is a necessity because of the action of the Holy Spirit. It is especially noted in the Acts of the Apostles. The mission of the church moves forward as the Holy Spirit pushes the boundaries in new ways not seen before.[6] We find in Acts that this reimagining takes place as new situations, new pictures, emerge in the pushing forward of the Holy Spirit within new cultures and civilizations. This was certainly the case in Peter's encounter with Cornelius in Acts 10. It required a re-envisioning and rethinking for Peter and the church as the Spirit brought forth new life and hope. But this re-envisioning required Peter, Paul, and others to witness not from the center but rather from the periphery of the church's mainline reading and practice. This is obvious in our reading of Acts. The re-envisioning of the proclamation of the gospel from the margins in the early church was due to the work of the Holy Spirit in the lives of the people.[7] This stand created a restlessness of the heart in their new standing and borderland experience in the ancient world.

My reimagining of the Reformation and the theology of justification is also carried out within a borderland experience. It is carried out in the midst of the large Latino population present and growing in the United States. It is tempered by my evangelical catholic faith that was first witnessed to me as a teenager and then further embedded in me by Lutheran seminaries grounded in Western European theology. It is read in the context of the faith of my Cuban

6. Justo L. González, *Acts: The Gospel of the Spirit* (Maryknoll, NY: Orbis, 2001), 8–10. Cf. Paul R. Hinlicky, *Luther and the Beloved Community: A Path for Christian Theology after Christendom* (Grand Rapids: Eerdmans, 2010), xvii–xviii. Hinlicky is conscious about the place and function of the Holy Spirit as the Spirit moves us forward in doing theology today.

7. Luther makes this point in his *Commentary on the Prophet Joel*. See "Preface to the Prophet Joel" (1532) (*LW* 45:318–19).

family, which formed me and gave me hope in the living God long before I could verbalize or realize it. This faith of my people resurrected in the restlessness of my heart during my first years of ministry in Chicago. This faith of my people is also informed by other faithful Caribbean and Latin American believers among whom I worked as a pastor in Chicago, Illinois, and Hollywood, Florida.

Anita de Luna, a Mexican American theologian who also grew up within a borderland experience of being a Mexican and an American, a Protestant and a Catholic, aptly explains how this faith experience from the margins is profoundly present among Latinos, Catholics and Protestants alike.[8] That is where the God of life is present and sustaining people. Luna offers in her study examples of how this living borderland faith is an integral part of Pentecostal as well as Catholic spirituality. This is significant in that the majority of US Latinos today consider themselves primarily Catholics or Pentecostals. At the same time it should be noted that this faith expression is rooted in a Catholic popular religiosity for most US Latinos, whether they are Catholic, Protestant, or Pentecostal.[9] This will be a crucial consideration and point of departure in the following section. There we will engage in a borderland reimagining of the doctrine of justification in light of US Latino popular religiosity. This is not the only locus where we are able to engage in this reimagining. It is, however, the crucial locus for discovering how a Latino reimagining of the Reformation needs to be grounded in a

8. Anita de Luna, "Popular Religion and Spirituality," in *Handbook of Latina/o Theologies*, ed. Edwin David Aponte and Miguel A. De La Torre (St. Louis: Chalice, 2006), 3–4.

9. Luna, "Popular Religion and Spirituality," 108–11. This has been my experience as well as the experience of Luna, who grew up Presbyterian and Catholic. Pope Francis's pastoral theology is also grounded in a similar perspective. His vision of evangelization begins with the "popular religiosity of the people." This was at the center of his pastoral work in Argentina, long before this was articulated among US Latino theologians. The religious and cultural experience from the people is crucial for his pastoral practice. See Allan Figueroa Deck, *Francis, Bishop of Rome* (New York: Paulist, 2016), 44–59.

strong affirmation of life. This focus always begins from the context of the everyday lives of people.

Now, however, we need to engage a crucial question for this study: why is the Reformation re-reading of the gospel from the margins tempered by a strong affirmation of life? US Latinos, whether they were born in the United States or came to the country through migration, live in displacement, dislocation between two cultures, two ways of life. This state has sometimes been described as living in the diaspora. The diaspora is also, in the words of Luis Rivera-Pagán, "an important object of critical analysis because it is the social historical context of many displaced Third World peoples."[10] In this pilgrim state of dislocation and displacement, the re-reading of the gospel entails a painful process in articulating our two world experiences in light of the God of life.

I must emphasize at this juncture that our whole being (social and personal) is restless in our quest for life in the midst of historical displacement. This is our human condition. This is how Virgilio Elizondo identifies this quest in the diaspora: "The deepest suffering of the mestizo comes from what we might call an 'unfinished identity,' or better yet, an undefined one. One of the core needs of human beings is the existential knowledge that regardless of who I am socially or morally, I am."[11] This "I am" is not a mere personal and existential "I am."[12] Before I could think or rationalize my life, my "I am" was already being shaped and formed by the care of my mother, father, and grandparents, and the community in which I grew up.

---

10. Luis N. Rivera-Pagán, *Essays from the Margins* (Eugene, OR: Cascade, 2014), 47–52.

11. Virgilio Elizondo, "Mestizaje as a Locus of Theological Reflection," in *Beyond Borders: Writings of Virgilio Elizondo and Friends*, ed. Timothy Matovina (Maryknoll, NY: Orbis, 2000), 162–63.

12. The experience of rejection within our borderland is what disrupts and limits our identity. Typical existential questions are born out of our life-limit questions such as questions about death, freedom, and guilt. This is not what Elizondo is describing here as our "unfinished identity."

This does not mean that my community or other Latino communities are or were utopias free from sin and evil. My identity and life were also forged within the sin and restlessness that inhabit our land and our souls. Latinos had and have our own struggles with sin and evil in our homelands. However, as we migrated and became aware that we were members of a community regarded as "foreign," our way of life became deeply challenged. We found that we were no longer welcome to all that life had to offer in the new community where we lived and had our being. This is very much present in the public rhetoric of the United States today. Poor Latinos are abused and mistreated like indentured servants while being denied the right to live and exist in the United States. There is great abuse, mistreatment, and racism directed today against US Hispanic immigrants. The color brown has become ever more suspect and rejected today in North American society. Also, we, poor or educated alike, are not considered seriously, treated as tokens, or worse, ignored within the inner sanctum of our Christian denominations as they make policy or plan for the mission of the church.

This compels us within our state of dislocation and ambiguity, our marginality, to reimagine God's active presence among us as the God of life. What is at stake in this hermeneutical and epistemological shift for our reimagining of the gospel of the Reformation? Our starting point is from life itself. Latino and Latina theologians understand this point of departure as living *en lo cotidiano*. Walter Mignolo expresses succinctly the different starting points for an epistemology grounded in modernity and border thinking:

> "I am where I think" becomes the starting point, the historical foundation of border thinking and decolonial doing. While "I think, therefore, I am" focuses on the "I think" and disregards the "I am," the formula "I am where I think" highlights the "I," not a "new" universal "I," but an "I" that dwells in the border and has been marked by the colonial wound.[13]

13. Mignolo, *Local Histories/Global Designs*, xiv. See my comments in note 12.

This reading conforms to a Reformation hermeneutics that believes that God speaks the good news of life in the midst of death to a community with restless hearts.[14] The reading of the holy text springs forth from our life situations. This text is not an esoteric message to be read and understood only by a privileged few (i.e., by the enlightened experts or the theologians). During the Reformation a significant step was taken when the faithful were encouraged to read and meditate on the Holy Scriptures. They could find solace in the Word through the reading and application of the text within their life situations. This Word had the authority of the Holy Spirit. The teachings of the clergy were not disdained (at least in most Reformation quarters), but these professional interpreters were not the only preservers or interpreters of the faith.[15]

The Reformation affirmation of the importance of the priesthood of all believers in the reading of Scripture, however, was marred by modernism. A superior and intellectual reading of the texts was preferred over the reading of the baptized and faithful communities of faith. Sadly, these claims were disguised further in the name of Christianity to disdain the indigenous cultures of Latin America and Africa in order to establish dominance over those cultures.[16] This

14. See Jean-Pierre Ruiz, "The Word Became Flesh and the Flesh Becomes Word: Notes toward a U.S. Latino/a Theology," in *Building Bridges, Doing Justice: Constructing a Latino/a Ecumenical Theology*, ed. Orlando E. Espín (Maryknoll, NY: Orbis, 2009), 53–59. Pierre-Ruiz's point of departure is the restlessness of our hearts because we live at the margins.

15. See Martin Luther, "Sermons on the First Epistle of Saint Peter" (*LW* 30:54–56). Luther comments that the vocation of the priesthood of all believers is living a cruciform existence in prayer, proclamation, and a life of service to others. This office is exercised in the community of faith, where "they all have this office [the priesthood of all believers] but nobody has any more authority than the other person has" (55). Cf. Jean-Pierre Ruiz, *Readings from the Edges: The Bible and People on the Move* (Maryknoll, NY: Orbis, 2011), where one will find the importance of the readings of the texts by the priesthood of all believers of the diaspora and at the margins for our Christian lives.

16. See Enrique Dussel, *The Invention of the Americas* (New York: Continuum,

claim still exists in those who insist that professional interpretations from the dominant culture are the only correct readings of the text. Our borderland pilgrimage and experience are inconsequential to the reading of the biblical texts. Those who hold this claim will find the project in this book (reimagining the Reformation in light of a borderland experience) to be backward, unscholarly, without rigor, and inconsequential to Reformation or Luther studies. Their claim invalidates the gift of the Spirit given to the priesthood of all believers in reading the Holy Scriptures for and within our communities of faith. It also invalidates the centrality for Christian persons and Christian communities of listening to God's Word in their everyday lives.[17] This claim is also contrary to the Reformation spirit and Luther. In the words of Luther: "For one becomes a theologian by living, by dying, by being damned: not by mere intellectualizing, reading, and speculating."[18]

It is right and salutary to take note of the many faithful Luther scholars and church historians who have spent great time and effort to show the relevancy of the Reformation teaching of justification by faith for our times. They concentrate mainly on addressing the restlessness of their traditional communities of faith. I have gathered many insights from them throughout the years. However, in spite of their faithful undertakings, I find that their Western European theological positioning seeks mainly to give clarity to the Reformation witness in light of questions posed by modernity and faith questions arising from their European or North American theological con-

---

1995), and Lamin Sanneh, *Religion and the Variety of Culture* (Valley Forge, PA: Trinity, 1996).

17. Oswald Bayer, *Martin Luther's Theology: A Contemporary Interpretation*, trans. Thomas H. Trapp (Grand Rapids: Eerdmans, 2008), 15-28. Carmen Nanko-Fernández, *Theologizing in Espanglish* (Maryknoll, NY: Orbis, 2010), points out how important this reading is for pastoral theology and also how the theological academy as well as mainstream church leaders ignore or downplay this reading from below.

18. The quote is from Luther's *Operationes in Psalmos* (1519-21) (*WA* 5:163.29-30). My translation from the Latin. See also Bayer, *Martin Luther's Theology*, 30-32.

cerns.[19] Our borderland questions of faith are nonexistent in their theological equations. This is not a judgment but a concern in light of the sign of the times. Lutheran theologians and scholars doing theology in the United States can no longer ignore the borderland disjunction present in our Latino communities of faith. For that matter, our borderland restlessness cannot be ignored any longer by theologians of other Protestant and evangelical traditions.

The Latin American and Caribbean worlds' restlessness of heart, and the rich questions and concerns that they offer, are an ever-growing reality in North America. In fact, the Latino identity and conscience continues to be a living torch in the life and souls of second- and third-generation US Latinos.[20] A growing Latino population is here to stay and live, evoking and acting on the restlessness of their hearts whether we want this to be or not. This identity and restlessness has become a sore spot within national politics and North American churches. This is why it is imperative to re-vision and reimagine the Reformation in light of a Latino borderland experience. It is critical for an evangelical catholic witness in the United States. It is also crucial to engage other ethnic groups in the United States and the world. Present ecumenical documents and dialogues understand the urgency of this task.[21]

---

19. See Bayer, *Martin Luther's Theology*; Christine Helmer, ed., *The Global Luther: A Theologian for Modern Times* (Minneapolis: Fortress, 2009); Robert Kolb, Irene Dingel, and L'Ubomír Batka, eds., *The Oxford Handbook of Martin Luther's Theology* (Oxford: Oxford University Press, 2014).

20. See Daniel A. Rodriguez, *A Future for the Latino Church: Witness for Multilingual, Multigenerational Hispanic Congregations* (Downers Grove, IL: InterVarsity, 2011), 54; Samuel P. Huntington, *Who Are We? The Challenges to America's National Identity* (New York: Simon and Schuster, 2004), 242–43.

21. Lutheran World Federation and the Pontifical Council for Promoting Christian Unity, *From Conflict to Communion: Lutheran-Catholic Common Commemoration of the Reformation in 2017* (Leipzig: Evangelische Verlagsanstalt, 2013), 13–14.

The Centrality of Justification

The gospel and the witness of justification by faith are crucial to the reimagining of the Reformation faith. The article of justification has been an urgent topic for discussion in our most recent ecumenical dialogues. The ecumenical document *From Conflict to Communion*, signed by representatives of the Catholic Church and the Lutheran World Federation (LWF) to commemorate the Reformation in 2017, acknowledges the witness of the gospel of Jesus Christ as the center of the Christian faith. This document also affirms as the guiding rule of this witness the doctrine of justification:[22] "We take as our guiding rule the doctrine of justification, which expresses the message of the gospel and therefore 'constantly serves to orient all the teachings and practice of our churches to Christ.'"[23]

Alister McGrath offers several reasons why the doctrine of justification by faith should occupy a central focus today for the Christian witness of the church in "Justification as a Hermeneutical Principle."[24] This is his concluding essay in *Iustitia Dei*, volume 2, the second part of his study on the history of the Christian doctrine of justification. Even though he wrote this essay in 1986, his observations are pertinent for the twenty-first century. McGrath affirms what I have gathered from other sources.

The doctrine of justification by grace plays a prominent role in the witness of the Christian church in the twenty-first century. This message continues to find a response among those who are addressed. We have already observed how it plays a prominent role in the ecumenical witness of Catholics and Lutherans. They have reached an important consensus (as well as with other Christian denominations) on the disputed questions of justification. It is clear

22. *FCTC*, 7 (see also 46). This document affirms what was already affirmed and proposed in the *Joint Declaration on the Doctrine of Justification* in 1999.

23. *FCTC*, 7.

24. Alister E. McGrath, *Iustitia Dei: A History of the Christian Doctrine of Justification*, 2 vols. (Cambridge: Cambridge University Press, 1986), 2:184–91.

also, as McGrath observes, that the development of the doctrine of justification indicates a general consensus of the church throughout the ages "to the effect that the human situation has been transformed [by] the action of God in Jesus Christ."[25] This action of God in transforming the human situation is grounded in the priority of the grace of God.[26]

McGrath also observes that the urgency and relevance of the doctrine of justification has an important role for the identity and existence of the Christian church. This requires, in his estimation, that we move beyond academic analysis to find how this doctrine takes form in the popular preaching and literature of the church.[27] It has become quite obvious how this is a crucial point of departure in the ecumenical affirmations and work of the church catholic. This is one of the most important foci of the document *From Conflict to Communion*.[28] But there is more. There is an earnest desire in light of this stand to find a vibrant incarnational witness of the gospel within the language, culture, and human struggles of people throughout the world. There is also a genuine desire to carry out a self-critical study of ourselves in a spirit of repentance.[29] This is why I consider the reimagining of the doctrine of justification in light of my borderland US Latino standing in the world and society crucial and relevant. It is crucial to the yearnings of our restless hearts as we seek to proclaim the God of life in the midst of violence and death.

Theodore Dieter in "Why Does Luther's Doctrine of Justifica-

25. McGrath, *Iustitia Dei*, 2:190. There is a debate, however, concerning the precise nature of this action and how it affects humanity. The only challenge to this consensus worth mentioning came from the Enlightenment. This challenge did not gain ground in the debates concerning the doctrine.

26. It is also generally understood that human beings are involved in some manner with God's justifying action. McGrath also finds this to be the case, and I agree, with the theologians of the *via moderna*.

27. McGrath, *Iustitia Dei*, 2:190.

28. *FCTC*, 13–14.

29. *FCTC*, 7, 13.

tion Matter Today?" brings us closer to the task at hand.[30] He offers in this essay an important quote from the Proceedings of the Fourth Assembly of the LWF that took place in Helsinki, July 30–August 11, 1963. This is how the document underlines the reimagining of the doctrine of justification for our times:

> The Reformation witness to justification by faith alone was the answer to the existential question: "How do I find a gracious God?" Almost no one asks this question in the world we live in today. But the question persists: "How do I find meaning for my life?" When man seeks for meaning in life he is impelled to justify his existence in his own eyes and before his fellow man. He then proceeds to judge his fellow men by these same standards. . . . It also explains why there is so much mutual accusation and condemnation. Do men not all compulsively pursue dreams of a future which they expect will give validity to their lives?[31]

The understanding of the God of our justification as the God of life was right up front and center already in the early 1960s among the world Lutheran leadership. Dieter cautions us, however, not to employ the doctrine of justification to find the solution to a basic problem within the human condition, or to address a few elementary aspects of human life (such as the problems of doubt, uncertainty, and social inequality).[32] I am in agreement with him that this often leads to mutual accusations and condemnations. The reason that this chapter is directed to understand the God of our justification as the God of life from a borderland experience is not

---

30. Theodore Dieter, "Why Does Luther's Doctrine of Justification Matter Today?" in *The Global Luther: A Theologian for Modern Times*, ed. Christine Helmer (Minneapolis: Fortress, 2009), 189–209.

31. Dieter, "Why Does Luther's Doctrine of Justification Matter Today?" 190.

32. Dieter, "Why Does Luther's Doctrine of Justification Matter Today?" 191. Hinlicky (*Luther and the Beloved Community*, 35–36) offers the same caution.

to engage in condemnation. Nor is it to give a preconceived fabricated answer to one problem within the human condition. My purpose is to give witness to the God of life in our present state of marginality and death. This is a crucial teaching present in Luther's affirmation of the God of creation as the God of redemption.[33] It has been explored by several Luther scholars. However, it has not been forcefully discussed or reimagined from the margins. This quest can only begin in the midst of the life that God created and continues to create (Acts 17:27–28).

Reimagining Justification from a Latino Borderland Locus

Lutherans tend to ask in true catechetical form: what does this mean? The question should be asked in this manner for this chapter: what does the doctrine of justification by faith mean within the borderland experience of US Latino communities? In particular, what does the doctrine of justification by faith mean within a US Latino popular religiosity borderland experience?

I offer as a first case study my father's (Antonio García) popular religiosity as a living example of what needs to be taken into account in our reimagining of the doctrine of justification from the margins. First of all, he understood that our righteousness comes from God. This is how he read Romans 3.[34] However, he never let go of the image and presence of San Lázaro in his life. This had to do with his borderland experience of being a Christian in exile. His popular religiosity had a lot to do with his faith. It was the starting point in

---

33. See Bayer, *Martin Luther's Theology*, 95–120. He has done an admirable job of showing this intricate and powerful connection in Luther. Luther's insights, however, need to be reimagined in light of the radical nature of the presence of God's righteousness in our marginality. This is what is discussed below.

34. My father read his Bible in Spanish. Note that these key texts in Romans are translated with *justicia* (justice) in Spanish to express the righteousness (*dikaiosynē*) of God.

his life to experience and express the righteousness of God. This righteousness affirms all of God's children as God walks with them. There were two things that characterized my father's double identity and consciousness. On the one hand he found in the proclamation of justification by faith a God who affirmed and made him worthy. On the other hand he found God in his righteousness walking with him in his daily struggles in a foreign land. He found his primary affirmation for his struggles in life through his popular religiosity.

I have many memories of conversations with my father concerning his feelings and struggles in these matters. I am also a witness to the many real situations that created his specific struggles for life within the diaspora. My father identified especially with the Lazarus of Luke 16:19-31. For him this Lazarus was a real person like him, whom God declared and affirmed a worthy person, despite his poverty, sin, and human condition. Lazarus is called by his real name and is identified as a worthy person in God's eyes. This image has also been powerfully present among exiled Salvadorans in the United States.[35] The God of our justification is ever present as the God who gives and affirms life in this popular religious image. In this gift of righteousness, God transforms and gives new life in the power of the Holy Spirit to his creation.[36]

San Lázaro is not, however, the predominant image in the popular religiosity of Latinos in the United States and Latin America. The most compelling image is the Virgen de Guadalupe. Many US Latino and Latina theologians have reflected on their borderland identity and meaning in light of the Virgen de Guadalupe. It is central to their Christian borderland experience and duality

---

35. Harold Recinos, "The Barrio as a Locus of a New Church," in *Hispanic/Latino Theology*, ed. Ada María Isasi-Díaz and Fernando Segovia (Minneapolis: Fortress, 2000), 186-87. Recinos emphasizes how this image denotes among US Hispanics in the city the figure of the crucified Christ.

36. See Samuel Solívan, "Sources of a Hispanic/Latino American Theology: A Pentecostal Perspective," in *Hispanic/Latino Theology*, ed. Ada María Isasi-Díaz and Fernando Segovia (Minneapolis: Fortress, 2000), 137-41.

of being.[37] For our purposes, however, we will concentrate on the works of Virgilio Elizondo and Pedro Alarcón Méndez.[38]

Virgilio Elizondo eloquently describes in his essay "People Resurrect at Tepeyac" how the narrative and event of the Virgin of Guadalupe affirms the presence of the God of life in the borderland experience of Mexican and Mexican American people:

> Equally, one cannot appreciate the full salvific and redemptive force of Guadalupe without seeing it in the full context of the historical moment in which it took place. Guadalupe is not an apparition, but a major intervention of God's liberating power in history. It is an Exodus and a Resurrection event of an enslaved and dying people. The God of freedom liberates from the strongest possible government and this same God of life raises to new life what human beings seek to kill. Guadalupe is truly an epiphany of God's love at the precise moment when abandonment by God has been experienced by the people at large.[39]

Elizondo claims that the Guadalupe story is the first real anthropological translation and proclamation of the gospel to the people of the Americas. He also claims that this is why upon seeing and hearing this story, millions have responded in faith. What does this story bring to play in our reimagining of the Reformation gospel? First of all, God's declaration of his redeeming righteousness cannot be separated from his presence in creation. Otherwise, we diminish the creative power of God's presence. Those acquainted with the Guadalupan narrative remember that the Virgen de Guadalupe presents herself to Juan Diego, speaking to him in his native lan-

37. See Jeanette Rodríguez, *Our Lady of Guadalupe* (Austin: University of Texas Press, 2005). There are hundreds of books written on this subject.

38. Virgilio Elizondo, *The Future Is Mestizo: Life Where Cultures Meet* (Boulder: University Press of Colorado, 2000), 57–66; P. Pedro Alarcón Méndez, *El Amor de Jesús vivo en la Virgen de Guadalupe* (Bloomington, IN: Palibrio, 2013).

39. Elizondo, *The Future Is Mestizo*, 59.

guage of Nahuatl. Guadalupe communicates God's message of love and affirmation for his mestizo people to Juan Diego. Juan Diego must announce this message of good news to the bishop.

When he presents himself to the bishop, Juan Diego finds fault in himself because of the bishop's unwillingness to hear his message. In other words, Juan Diego is confronted with his borderland reality in witnessing to the gospel. He is declared worthy by God because he is chosen to convey God's message to the bishop. God's care is to be powerfully present among his people at Tepeyac in the presence of his mother (María) Guadalupe. Juan Diego also regards the bishop as the proper authority in communicating God's message to his mestizo people. The bishop, however, does not listen to Juan Diego the first time. The message finally is understood and realized in the miracle created by the Virgen de Guadalupe. This message is that God cares about and is faithful to his covenant and promises made to his people. This is why God affirms the worthiness of Juan Diego through his own mother Mary. The bishop finally acknowledges and is transformed by God's word of life within the margins. He now acknowledges how God acts in creating new life out of death. In terms of my evangelical catholic faith this narrative needs to be reimagined and understood in light of God's declaration of his righteousness and justice for all his people. I realize how this narrative has been used to direct readers toward an adoration of Mary. But this is not the real intention and meaning of this narrative.

I call evangelical and Protestant Christians, therefore, to be careful not to simply reject this narrative as unbiblical. If we do so, we are in fact rejecting the meaning of Mary's Song in Luke 1:46–54. Luther himself identified the mother of God, the mother of Christ, as an important bearer and magnifier of the gospel to the poor and the powerful (what US Latinos affirm as the people of the borderland): "So this word 'magnifies' is used by Mary to indicate what her hymn of praise is to be about, namely, the great works and deeds of God, for the strengthening of our faith, for the comforting of all those of low degree, and for the terrifying of all the mighty ones of earth."[40] The righteousness of God cannot be separated from God's creative acts of love and justice in Mary's Song. This is parallel and congruent to the narrative of the Virgen de Guadalupe. This is the role that is affirmed and understood by Pedro Alárcon Méndez concerning Guadalupe in the life of the mestizo: "The Virgen de Guadalupe connects us to the biblical text in a general and particular manner, in the way that Mary lives a faith that sings the Magnificat and foresees God's merciful actions to reconfigure the *náhuatl* world, devastated at its very roots and in this manner reconfigured."[41]

There is in this vision the priority of Holy Scripture, and the realization that it is the gospel that leads to our faith in Christ, which is essential to our salvation. The event at Tepeyac, as it is narrated in the *Nican Mopohua*,[42] Alarcón Méndez argues, is a sign of the acceptance and reception of the gospel by indigenous cultures in light of their borderland situation. It contributes to a reimagining and rediscovery of the gospel, where the centrality of our faith in the living Christ lives within our borderland identity in constructing a new way of life. This way of life honors the presence of the living God in his creation because of the vitality of his righteousness and justice. God calls worthy those who are ignored in the margins. He transforms their situation by offering in his word of mercy also his word of justice. This point of departure is, in light of my US Latino borderland life, at the center of our reimagining of our Reformation faith.

40. Martin Luther, "The Magnificat," in *The Sermon on the Mount and the Magnificat* (*LW* 21:306).

41. Méndez, *El Amor de Jesús vivo y la Virgen de Guadalupe*, 13. My translation from Spanish. Cf. Eldín Villafañe, *The Liberating Spirit: Toward an Hispanic American Pentecostal Social Ethic* (Grand Rapids: Eerdmans, 1993), 52–57. Villafañe, a Pentecostal theologian, offers similar insights.

42. The *Nican Mopohua* was written in Náhuatl. It contains the story of the apparitions of the Virgin of Guadalupe at Tepeyac in 1531. The original date and authorship is in dispute. The document dates back to the late sixteenth century. See Miguel León-Portilla, *Tonatzín Guadalupe: Pensamiento náhuatl y pensamiento cristiano en el "Nicanmopohua"* (México, D.F.: Fondo de Cultura Económica, 2000).

Reading Justification by Faith in Spanish

Romans 1:17 played a crucial role in the rediscovery of the gospel for Luther. His heart was restless because he could not understand at first whether God was threatening us with his wrath or was offering his grace and mercy with his word of righteousness. In the words of Luther, he "meditated day and night on this matter."[43] Now we meditate on the meaning of this text in Spanish. "For in it the righteousness [*iustitia*; *justicia*] of God is revealed through faith for faith; as it is written, 'The one who is righteous [*iustus*; *justo*] will live by faith.'" We cannot help but notice that the word "righteousness" in both Spanish and Latin is translated as "justice." What kind of justice or righteousness is this? During Luther's early ministry, his reading of this text, as well as of other Pauline texts that affirmed God's righteousness (*dikaiosynē*), was understood in terms of retributive justice. There are several factors that led to this.[44]

In terms of Western thinking the sense of justice as retributive rather than commutative prevailed. The Western church depended on Latin translations of Scripture during most of the first 1,500 years of its theological work. The sense of *iustitia Dei* (God's justice) and *iustificare* (to justify) derived from a judicial understanding of retributive justice.[45] God's justice was understood in

43. James Kittelson, *Luther the Reformer: The Story of the Man and His Career* (Minneapolis: Fortress, 1986), 134.

44. McGrath, *Iustitia Dei*, 1:8-14. It has to do with how the term "righteousness" (*ṣĕdāqâ*) was employed in the Hebrew and how it was appropriated in the LXX, the Greek translation of the Hebrew text. The Hebrew Scriptures employ the term *ṣĕdāqâ* as retributive (such as in Lev. 19:15; Ps. 31:2) or commutative (as in Ps. 112:9). The Hebrew term *ṣĕdāqâ* was hard to accommodate in the translation of the text into Greek in the LXX. The use of the term *dikaiosynē* for God's righteousness did not always fit the bill. In Psalm 71:2 we find that the Hebrew uses *ṣĕdāqâ*, the LXX *dikaiosynē*, and the Vulgate *justitia*. Justice definitely figures in the context of these two psalms with God's offer of mercy and grace. This was not the preferred reading of exegetes in Luther's day.

45. McGrath, *Iustitia Dei*, 1:7-10. This is due to the adoption of the juristic terminologies employed by Marcus Tullius Cicero and Justinian I.

the sense of a judgment declared by a judge in light of how people had acted in reference to the established law. This is how God's righteousness (*dikaiosynē*) was read and interpreted by Pauline scholars in reading his epistles in the twelfth century.[46] However, when Latinos and Latinas call for God's *justicia*, justice, they are not calling for God's wrath to be realized but rather for God to preserve them in his mercy from those who persecute them. This proclamation that the God of life is the God of justice was central to the witness of the martyr Archbishop Oscar Romero in El Salvador.[47] It was at the core of his proclamation of justification by faith. I am convinced through my studies that Luther understood the doctrine of justification in forensic terms.[48] But there is more to know and understand in Luther's appropriation of God's righteousness. However, I also believe that we can no longer pit a "forensic approach" against an "effective approach." I affirm, along the lines of Mark Mattes and his understanding of Luther's view of language, that God's Word actually alters and creates reality. God is present in renewing our reality. Mattes compares and finds a unified vision between the creative Word of God's forensic righteousness and the creative Word of God present in transforming

46. McGrath, *Iustitia Dei*, 1:3–15. He offers an excellent study and several examples of how the interpretation and understanding of the righteousness of God moved from *coram Deo* to *iustitia in hominibus*. He also offers examples of how this took place through the transference of the texts from Hebrew to Greek to Latin linguistic and cultural expressions.

47. See Jon Sobrino, *Archbishop Romero: Memories and Reflection* (Maryknoll, NY: Orbis, 1990), 148.

48. See Ricardo García-Villoslada, *Martín Lutero* (Madrid: Biblioteca de Autores Cristianos, 1973), 1:360–61. Garcia-Villoslada narrates a table talk in which Luther and Melanchthon discussed the topic of justification and whether it was through internal renewal or extrinsic through gracious imputation. Luther told Melanchthon the following: "I am completely certain that we are justified before God only through gracious imputation." Melanchthon continued to hammer Luther with questions concerning the topic and Luther continued to affirm that "man is justified and remains in that justification only through the mercy of God" (see *Tischreden*, 6727 6:149). My translation from the Spanish.

the world.[49] We cannot separate these two important dimensions of the righteousness of God.

The centrality of God's Word is the Word Incarnate. This is not the Greek *logos* but rather the active spoken Word of the Hebrew Scriptures. The active Verb of God at creation is present now with the same living action in God's work of redemption to bring us life (John 1:1-5). It is in this active creative Verb rather than a plain noun where we live and have our being (John 1:14). This is how it is understood and translated into Spanish: "Y el Verbo [Verb] se hizo carne [became flesh] y habitó entre nosotros" (RV).[50] In this way of thinking, God's Verb of righteousness is the same present active Word in his work of redemption and creation. What does this mean in light of a US Latino borderland point of departure?

When US Latinos affirm the presence of a Lazarus or the Virgin of Guadalupe in their lives, they are affirming the presence of God, who speaks and acts his justice among them. God's incarnate love is very much present in his acts of justice. During charismatic services when members of the congregation cry out the utterance and presence of the Holy Spirit among them, these expressions are congruent expressions to the presence of the living God within Catholic popular religiosity. They are recognizing and affirming the presence of the God of life in their desolation. God's justice is present where there seems to be no justice. This, of course, is not the only issue that

---

49. Mark Mattes, "Luther on Justification as Forensic and Effective," in *The Oxford Handbook of Martin Luther's Theology*, ed. Robert Kolb, Irene Dingel, and L'Ubomír Batka (Oxford: Oxford University Press, 2014), 265.

50. This is how it has been translated into Spanish in the many Reina Valera versions. The most current translation, the Reina Valera Contemporánea (Sociedades Bíblicas Unidas, 2009), committed a major faux pas by translating this verse *La Palabra* (the Word) instead of *el Verbo se hizo carne*. The use of *el Verbo* has been the accepted translation and reading of the text in Spanish since the first translation by Casiodoro de Reina of the Bible into Spanish in the sixteenth century. See Ruiz, "The Word Became Flesh," 47-52. US Latino and Latina biblical interpreters have a great affinity for the Gospel of John because they find there God in action as the God of life.

creates a restlessness of the heart among our US Latino population. There are also personal questions concerning our relationship with God. We cannot separate, however, the justice of God in redemption from the justice of God in creation. What is missing, then, from our current reading of justification? What is specifically needed in our reimagining of justification by faith?

One of the key questions that needs to be addressed in this reimagining is: how is the justification of the ungodly a legitimate and crucial component in the history and proclamation of Jesus of Nazareth? This is an ever-crucial question that has been posed in contemporary theological studies concerning the validity of the doctrine of justification. However, in terms of a US Latino borderland experience, it is also a very crucial question through a different lens. We turn to Virgilio Elizondo's reflection in the *Galilean Journey*.[51] This has become the classic pioneer interpretative work for US Latino and Latina theologians in addressing the meaning of Jesus of Nazareth from the margins. The proclamation acts of Jesus of Galilee, the Son of God, in the Gospels are crucial to our proclamation of God's love and justice in the context of our borderland existence. The righteousness of God is synonymous with his mercy. Jesus renders his mercy and justice as he acts. This justice and righteousness is superior to human acts of righteousness (Matt. 5:20). However, they are proclaimed and grounded within the borderland experience of Galilee. We need to explore this theme by reflecting on the proclamation of God's righteousness in Matthew. This is a necessary step for the proclamation of the gospel within our Latino borderland.

The Gospel of Matthew uses the word "righteousness" (*dikaiosynē*) more often than any of the other Gospels—seven times.[52] It

---

51. Virgilio Elizondo, *Galilean Journey: The Mexican-American Promise* (Maryknoll, NY: Orbis, 1983), 54–58.

52. The Gospel of Luke uses the term only once (1:17). It is also used in Acts, which should be considered a continuation of Luke's Gospel, four times (10:35; 13:10; 17:31; 24:25), and in John twice (16:8; 16:10). It also appears in an adjectival form in Matthew 27:19. It does not appear in Mark.

is found primarily in the Sermon on the Mount, where the term appears five times, as a goal for followers of Jesus.[53] David Scaer asks a poignant question concerning what kind of righteousness Matthew proclaims in his Gospel: "Does the righteousness that is demanded of the followers of Jesus describe their behavior (living up to a code of right conduct) or is it superimposed on them from the outside by God for the sake of Jesus?"[54] God's bestowal of his righteousness is not a mere imperative to right moral conduct or a call for retributive justice. It is also more than a superimposed declarative gift from the outside. It is a living bestowal of his righteousness in action. It is an offer and gift of God's transformative renewal of our borderland experience.

The crucial question now is: what kind of righteousness was required in Matthew of followers of Jesus? Let's first explore Jesus's baptism in Matthew 3:15. We read: "Let it be so now, for thus it is fitting for us to fulfill all righteousness" (NRSV). What kind of righteousness is Jesus fulfilling? There are two possibilities. The traditional interpretation in Lutheranism is that Jesus is fulfilling the Law for us. Jesus stands on our behalf in completely fulfilling the Law for us. Echoes of this teaching are found in texts such as Romans 5:19. It can also be read another way. This fulfillment is not a mere fulfillment of right conduct on our behalf. It has to be read in relationship to Matthew 3:2. John the Baptist is proclaiming the presence and nearness of God's royal ruling in history. He realizes that Jesus is the bearer of this royal kingdom (Matt. 3:14). It is Jesus who fully brings forth, fully reveals in his ministry of reconciliation, the presence of God's kingdom and righteousness. The shocking news is that God's righteousness is already being unfolded in his mighty deeds of mercy and salvation (such as in Psalm 71; Isa. 51:5-8).[55]

---

53. David P. Scaer, *Discourses in Matthew: Jesus Teaches the Church* (St. Louis: Concordia, 2004), 245. Scaer offers an excellent discourse on "Righteousness in the Gospel of Matthew" (245-63) in his book.

54. Scaer, *Discourses in Matthew*, 245.

55. Jeffrey A. Gibbs, *Concordia Commentary on Matthew 1:1–11:1* (St. Louis:

Matthew 3:17–18 reveals the implication of Jesus's baptism in the fulfilling of all righteousness. Matthew narrates how the Holy Spirit immediately descended on Jesus and a voice from heaven (implying the Father) called Jesus "my Son, the Beloved, with whom I am well pleased." We find here echoes of Psalm 2, where the Anointed One of God is described as the Father's Son. In other words, Matthew acknowledges Jesus as God's Messiah, God's anointed one. He can also be identified as the servant of the Lord as it is expressed in Isaiah 42:1–4 and 61:1–9.[56] The words and image present in Isaiah 61:1–9 are quite significant in that Jesus proclaims them as his first message in the synagogue in Nazareth after his baptism (Luke 4:14–21). Clearly and inevitably Jesus's fulfilling of God's righteousness begins with his baptism. Jesus is anointed by the Spirit in order to bring forth and fulfill the righteousness that comes from God.[57] The followers of Jesus will be granted at their baptism this gift of the Holy Spirit (Matt. 3:11). This righteousness does not disdain the Law. It is not, however, the kind of righteousness that affirms a better and more precise following of the Law or moral principles. It is not a quantitative type of righteousness. The Pharisees and the teachers of the Law proclaimed a quantitative type of righteousness. Jesus calls for a greater righteousness. It is a qualitative one driven by the action of the God of life. It is one grounded on God's mercy to humanity.

This righteousness is identified in the life and proclamation of Jesus, the righteous one (Luke 23:47). It is not focused on an abstract uprightness and sovereignty of God. It is grounded on seeking first

---

Concordia, 2004), 180–84; Oscar Cullmann, *The Christology of the New Testament* (Philadelphia: Westminster, 1963), 66–68, 117–32.

56. Gibbs, *Concordia Commentary on Matthew 1:1–11:1*, 182.

57. This is why I concur with Scaer (*Discourses in Matthew*, 160) that Pilate's wife urges him to have nothing to do with that *dikaios* man. Unfortunately this text is more often translated as "innocent" man. The ESV translates it as "righteous" while the NRSV and the NIV translate it as "innocent" man. The Spanish translation uses the adjective *justo* (just, which is the same as righteous) in a consistent manner.

the kingdom of God and his righteousness (Matt. 6:33).[58] What does this righteousness entail? Listen to the Beatitudes in Matthew 5. It is a righteousness grounded in the passion of following Jesus Christ (v. 11). It is righteousness with a passion for God's creative life. It is the kind of righteousness that walks with the wounded and the frail (v. 6), seeking after reconciliation and peace (v. 9). It does not seek suffering or death but knows that this is the fate of Jesus's disciples who seek to bestow God's righteousness on the world (v. 11). In the final stage of his ministry Jesus reminds his disciples of this fact (20:24-27).

The Sermon on the Mount has mostly been interpreted as an ethical demand.[59] Modern commentaries usually point out that there are two definitions of righteousness. Matthew offers, in their assessment, a definition of righteousness that expresses "correct conduct" and Paul offers one that expresses God's righteousness as a "divine gift." Luther tends to follow this way of thinking. However, he was inconsistent. In Luther's explanation of the fourth Beatitude in Matthew 5:6 ("hunger and thirst for righteousness"), he interprets the righteousness in this verse as an outward righteousness before the world, a civil kind of righteousness.[60] At the same time Luther interprets the eighth Beatitude in Matthew 5:10 ("persecuted for righteousness' sake") as persecuted for Christ's sake, who himself

---

58. Scaer, *Discourses in Matthew*, 259. Scaer draws here from the exegetical work of W. D. Davies and Dale C. Allison Jr., *A Critical and Exegetical Commentary on the Gospel according to Saint* Matthew (Edinburgh: T&T Clark, 1988-97), 661.

59. Scaer (*Discourses in Matthew*, 250-58) also provides a short but enlightened study that supports the notion that in the early church Matthew and Paul were pillars in the teaching and catechesis of the church. This study will affirm that the righteousness affirmed by Matthew is one that comes from God as a gift and not through a mere ethical rigor and affirmation of God's Law.

60. Martin Luther, "The Sermon on the Mount," in *The Sermon on the Mount and the Magnificat* (*LW* 21:26). "Righteousness" in this passage must not be taken in the sense of the principal righteousness by which a person becomes acceptable to God.

is our righteousness.[61] This last interpretation is consistent with Luther's teaching on the "joyous exchange."

The clearest and most profound teaching of Luther on the dynamic presence of the God of our justification is found in his understanding of the "joyous exchange." This is an incarnational reality that must become ours in our appropriation of Christ's alien righteousness. In the act of faith this reality becomes ours. Not only does Christ receive our sins and our unrighteousness but we receive the righteousness of Christ in a real formal (*formaliter*) sense. Through this *admirabile commercium* ("joyous exchange") Christ empties himself (*exinanivit*) and pours into us (*indueret*) his qualities.[62] It is important to understand that under this "joyous exchange" we truly appropriate Christ's righteousness for our lives of faith. We incorporate into our lives the realization that, in spite of being totally sinful (*totus peccator*), we are also in Christ totally justified (*totus iustus*). This righteousness of faith in Luther's thought is not merely forensic as we find in the Age of Orthodoxy.[63] It is truly an "effective righteousness." Here Luther moves from explaining how Christ took the wrath of God and our sin to the theme of the appropriation of the living righteousness of Christ (alien as it may be) in our living faith. Luther affirms "what a "joyous exchange [this is] for our sins are not ours, but they are Christ's, and Christ's righteousness is not Christ's righteousness but rather it is our righteousness."[64] In the

---

61. Luther, "The Sermon on the Mount," in *The Sermon on the Mount and the Magnificat* (LW 21:46–47).

62. Martin Luther, *Operationes in Psalmos* (WA 5:607–8); and *Select Works of Martin Luther*, 4 vols., trans. Henry Cole (London: T. Bensley, 1924–26), 4:368–69. Here Luther is commenting on Psalm 22:1.

63. Regin Prenter, *Spiritus Creator*, trans. John M. Jensen (Philadelphia: Muhlenberg, 1953), 39–41. The works of Lutheran Protestant scholars such as Marc Lienhard, *Luther: Witness to Jesus Christ*, trans. Edwin H. Robertson (Minneapolis: Augsburg, 1983), 134–36, and Wilfred Joest, *Ontologie der Person bei Luther* (Göttingen: Vandenhoeck & Ruprecht, 1967), 373–75, as well as others, support this claim.

64. My translation from the Latin: "quod admirabili commertio peccata nos-

words of Regin Prenter: "Our alien righteousness is to Luther the living personal Christ, not a certain abstract contribution to faith."[65] In terms of our reimagining of the doctrine of justification for a proclamation of the God of life in our borderlands, the Catholic theologian Joseph Lortz poignantly summarizes what this means:

> Of course justification does mean that the "alien justice" of Christ is given to me by God through faith. According to Luther God makes it become my justice. Its origins and essence are external to me, but to the degree that God can become man, it becomes man's inner possession, which though in no way negates its nature as pure gift. . . . God does not merely make promises, but He communicates Himself.[66]

This communication is a real incarnate communication and not a mere speaking of God's promises.[67] It is necessary to find in this realization the walking of the crucified and risen Christ among us. Luther's affirmation of the "joyous exchange" in this context, I believe, affirms this incarnational presence. The Christian believer is offered in Christ a higher kind of righteousness as a gift of grace.

---

tra, iam non nostra, sed Christi sunt, etiustitia Christi non Christi, sed nostra est" (WA 5:608, 6-14).

65. Prenter, Spiritus Creator, 49.

66. Joseph Lortz, "The Basic Elements of Luther's Intellectual Life," in Catholic Scholars Dialogue with Luther, ed. Jared Wicks (Chicago: Loyola University Press, 1972), 17.

67. Cf. Bayer, Martin Luther's Theology, 229-30, and Hinlicky, Luther and the Beloved Community, 81-82. I believe that Hinlicky is on the right track concerning the "joyous exchange." However, the presence is more than a word of promise. It is Jesus walking with us in our struggles and marginality. Hinlicky and other Western thinkers pursue this topic from a subject and object understanding and rationality. I am not convinced that the language of mysticism is the right language to express this incarnational walking. It is real and Jesus walks with us in our need and vulnerable state. I read this in the way I already explained—how Jesus is present among us as Verb in John 1:14.

This brings us to a real case study for our consideration. What witness would the church give to María, who knows that Christ died for her sins but is ready to be deported back to her motherland? What would you do if she and her children are hungry and in need of help? I have heard Lutheran pastors in my denomination and other Christian denominations say, "She is getting what she deserves. She is breaking the law. She should go home. We should not help her or minister to her because she has broken the law in our country." If we follow a mere quantitative rather than qualitative proclamation of God's righteousness, our hearts will be unmoved. Meanwhile María holds on to her precious Virgencita. María knows by faith that God's forgiving mercy walks with her in new and strange places. God declares her unconditionally a somebody rather than a nobody, in his offer of precious, abundant life. This is why our offer of justification by faith must be reimagined. We are declared worthy through God's action in Christ. This offer and affirmation of righteousness is what should direct us in affirming the daily life of María as a child of God. It is in fact what Jesus of Nazareth embodied and proclaimed from his borderland, Nazareth of Galilee.

An excellent parallel biblical passage for our consideration is found in Matthew 1:18–25. It is in verse 19 that the word "righteous" first appears in the Gospel. The text reads: "Her husband Joseph, being a righteous [*dikaios*][68] man and unwilling to expose her to public disgrace, planned to dismiss her quietly." This text suggests a moral interpretation in that Joseph wants to follow the Law meticulously. But here we find that Joseph is deemed righteous because he wants to dismiss his wife quietly. In other words, he is merciful and wants to show mercy. This is his real intent. The announcement revealed to Mary concerning the work of God is reiterated again to Joseph by an angel. God is the one acting his gift of grace on her.

Now Joseph finds himself in a crisis. He knows what the right

68. Here *dikaios* expresses in adjectival form what the noun *dikaiosynē* articulates concerning Jesus in Matthew 27:19.

course of action is if he is to live within the mainline tradition of his community of faith. However, the angel proclaims to Joseph God's gift of grace to Mary and the world in the power of the Holy Spirit. Joseph is summoned to live in this radical offer of God's mercy and righteousness by taking Mary home as his bride (with all the rights and privilege of a worthy bride). In other words, while the Sermon on the Mount has not yet been proclaimed, Joseph hungers and thirsts for God's righteousness by being merciful, by being pure of heart (i.e., not double-minded), and by being willing to be persecuted for God's righteousness.

God declared Mary worthy through his gift to Mary. Joseph must now, through faith in God's action, affirm the worthiness bestowed on Mary. Joseph took Mary as his wife (Matt. 1:24). Now Joseph stands in this narrative affirming God's righteousness by doing something more radical and just in the Spirit of God's love. He is now willing to live with Mary in the margins. He now accepts the consequences as he welcomes Mary into the cradle of his family. Joseph is single-minded in his offer of God's righteousness to Mary. This is more than an acceptance of Mary. It is a new pattern of expressing God's redemptive love to his community. God's declaration of Mary's worthiness (which is his very own act of declaration and offer of mercy) is what lives in Joseph's act of binding reconciliation.

Gustavo Gutiérrez in his important study *The God of Life* reimagines the teaching of justification by affirming the God of life.[69] In his essay "The Ethics of the Kingdom," he reflects on the Beatitudes in the Sermon on the Mount. He, like Scaer, finds that in the Sermon on the Mount "righteousness is linked to the order of gift and gratuitousness."[70] Gutiérrez notes that the righteousness in

69. Gutiérrez, *The God of Life*, 118–45. Cf. Ada María Isasi-Díaz, *La Lucha Continues: Mujerista Theology* (Maryknoll, NY: Orbis, 2004), 219–39. She describes in particular how our life of reconciliation is an intrinsic element of justice.

70. Gutiérrez, *The God of Life*, 119. Here he quotes and affirms Christian Duquoc's insights on this.

question "is not limited to obeying precepts but draws its inspiration from an ever imaginative love."[71] He does not find, therefore, in the Sermon on the Mount that the priority for Jesus's disciples is to promote a moral ethics of God's kingdom. Gutiérrez, moreover, affirms a radical newness of God's righteousness in the Beatitudes. This righteousness demonstrates the dynamic presence of God's creative and imaginative love. He also identifies a common parallel and purpose in Matthew and Luke. A number of exegetical scholars find that Matthew spiritualizes the Beatitudes in places where Luke makes concrete historical statements about the Messiah. These exegetes conclude that Matthew turns the Beatitudes into purely interior and unincarnated dispositions. Gutiérrez (like me) disagrees with this conclusion. He observes: "Matthew retains the richness and complexity of the term 'justice' [= "righteousness"] in the Bible. Justice is the work God does and must also be the work of those who believe in God."[72]

God's righteousness entails the dynamic presence of the God of life in his redemption and creation. Gutiérrez is in tune in his reading of Matthew with the personal relationship that each believer needs to have with God. However, the faithful as the people of God must exercise concretely the presence of God's justice in the world.[73] It is more than plain ethical good works. It involves the presence of the God of life in his righteousness with the poor and the marginalized. They are declared worthy and accompanied

71. Gutiérrez, *The God of Life*, 119.

72. Gutiérrez, *The God of Life*, 120.

73. Cf. McGrath, *Iustitia Dei*, 1:33-35. McGrath pursues this idea in the political theology of Augustine's *Civitas Dei* (*City of God*). Augustine's concept of justice (*iustitia*) within the *civitas Dei* is based on the concept of God as *iustissimus ordinator*, who orders the universe according to his will. This is what Augustine urges the Christian community to affirm and act in the world and society. Augustine had a preoccupation similar to the one I have expressed. Unfortunately, his preoccupation in this matter is overshadowed by Neo-Platonism. Augustine's submission to God's will, as McGrath observes, "may reflect the neo-Platonist notion of the established order of the universe" (*Iustitia Dei*, 1:35).

by our righteous God in his offer of abundant life. God walks with them, as we also walk with them as little Christophers (bearers of Christ's righteousness)[74] in the borderland. Ethical rightness is not our guiding light. God's righteousness in his living presence is what guides our presence and sustains us within the duplicities present in our borderland. This is what Gutiérrez calls for in the manifestation of God's dynamic righteousness through the presence of God's imaginative living love. Living in light of this imaginative love calls for the transformation of our private and public spaces in living God's *justicia*, God's righteousness, in our time. This is the call that is made to Christians to carry out and act in light of God's declaration of his righteousness as the God of life. It is in this call that I find a powerful reimagining of the Reformation doctrine of justification for our time, our place, and our marginality.

---

74. This is what Luther actually calls Christian disciples under the cross who are living the "joyous exchange." See "Sermon at Coburg on Cross and Suffering" (*LW* 51:198; *WA* 32:29.18–21). This is also driven home in Luther's treatise *The Freedom of a Christian* (1520) (*LW* 31:367–68): "Each one should become as it were a Christ to the other that we may be Christs to one another and Christ may be the same in all."

CHAPTER 2

Justification and Eco-Justice

A Postcolonial Framework

Martin Luther's realization and appropriation of the divine justice that justifies was rooted in his quest for a gracious God. The salvation he sought God alone wrought through Jesus Christ's victory over sin, death, and the devil. All who claim by faith the promises of God revealed in Christ (*solus Christus*) are made right with God (justification); are delivered from those forces that had driven them, as Luther declaimed, "down to the deepest pit of despair";[1] and in the Spirit's power actuate themselves rightly in words and deeds of justice. While the domain for Luther's spiritual condition of condemnation was experienced primarily as individual interiority, this chapter proposes a Lutheran framework for interpreting conditions of communal exteriority among humans searching for divine justice in postcolonial settings of poverty. No theological anthropology, moreover, exists in isolation from context, environment, nature, and ecology—especially in a highly pluralistic, materialist, interconnected, politicized twenty-first-century global commons. Those seeking a gracious God and Savior—a deliverer from that which has driven them "down to the deepest pit of despair"—will encounter liberating truth through a consideration of

1. *The Bondage of the Will* (*LW* 33:217).

their bondage within the structural sin exerted on them by economic and ecological evil.

The prefix "eco-" is commonly and most functionally related to matters of ecology. For this postcolonial consideration, I extend its use to financial economies as well. I suggest this for two reasons: (1) economic globalization and environmental concerns are experienced in common as entwined and oppressive in postcolonial settings; and (2) there is a similar Greek grammatical usage of "eco-" for "economy" (*oikos*, household, and *nemomai*, to manage) and for "ecology" (as in the study of, *logos*), in this case, the study of God's household, or the created order.

In the Christian tradition, this global house is understood and affirmed as the locus for justice to be pursued, the theater for good works to flourish creatively (Eph. 2:10), the real world in which "world-work" occurs. Luther's term is *weltlich*[2]—which has been variously translated as "secular" or "temporal." In other words, there is commonality in both the domain of experience and in the proximity of definition. This justification, realized and appropriated within the realm of communal exteriority, becomes the sphere in which God concretely works salvation by grace, in Jesus Christ (a first-century Palestinian-Jewish teacher), in time (ca. 30 CE) and space (Calvary, a suburb of Jerusalem), and the place where Christians—those who bear this Christ to the world—enact in love that world-work. Justification and justice comprise a fluid mutuality of interplay, not a binary or even sequential cause-and-effect.

To further this argument concerning the incarnational situatedness of all aspects of God's saving work among people, this chapter undertakes a phenomenological approach that compares and demonstrates the connectedness between seemingly disparate fields, in this case, relating justification by grace to concerns for economic and ecological justice. The hinge of comparison this follows is a Lutheran doctrine of structural sin informed by catechetical

2. *Die Stad, das istweltlich regiment* (*WA* 50:652).

ethics and concrete narratives from two workers in Lutheran communities located in postcolonial settings. The catechetical ethics dimension is grounded in Luther's teachings about the commandments, especially the first, fifth, seventh, ninth, and tenth. The Ten Commandments are correlated to the "structures of creation." Our world is grounded by God in Christ who is the Creator and Sustainer of all persons, all relationships, all systems—there are no unsupervised processes in the universe. Christ "himself is before all things, and in him all things hold together" (Col. 1:17).

In a world devastated by the fall into sin, there are no structures of creation that do not bear the mark of sinfulness. To deny this pervasiveness of sin is to deny both the gravity of the fall and the depth of Christ's sacrificial victory. Yet, sin impairs spiritual vision and reinforces an arrogant firmness, an internal hypocrisy that holds to structures—rather than Christ—religiously, idolizing traditions nostalgically, clinging to belief in systems without self-criticality, valiantly denying the reality of structures of sin while upholding institutional human innocence apart from corporate repentance. This constitutes a kind of fanaticism, according to Luther: "Christians never hold so steadfastly to Christ as . . . fanatics hold to their teaching, for although Christians also continue to believe until they die, yet they often stumble and begin to doubt. This is not so in the case of fanatics, who stand firm."[3] Such sophisticated self-righteousness camouflages the sins of powerbrokers, of possessors of privilege, including colonizers. The Lutheran Confessions themselves are replete with cross-cutting, countercultural critique applicable to all people: "This last commandment, therefore, is not addressed to those whom the world considers wicked rogues, but precisely to the most upright—to people who wish to be commended as honest and virtuous because they have not offended against the preceding commandments."[4]

---

3. "Table Talk" (*LW* 54:454).
4. *Large Catechism* (*BC*, 426).

An analysis of structural sin, therefore, serves as a mediating link for considering the correlation between justification and justice since a common thread consists in the problem of evil. A goal of this approach is to join with those who have, as Robert Kolb summarizes, "striven to demonstrate that Luther's proclamation of the God who justifies is not trapped inside sixteenth century thought forms but is relevant and applicable to the dilemmas and distresses of the twenty-first century."[5] In that sense, readers will encounter nothing new here, but rather a reiteration of ancient truth revealed in the living tradition of Scripture alone (*sola Scriptura*) in a manner that creatively disrupts the wounding captivity of traditionalism. To be evocative of Jaroslav Pelikan, creative disruption functions best when it is creative with respect to tradition (the deceased's living faith) and disruptive with respect to traditionalism (the dead faith of those who are alive).[6]

In a manner similar to the approach taken by anthropological research—utilizing an ethnographical model that emphasizes a direct relational encounter with cultural phenomena—this chapter presents two accounts directly from Lutherans working in Africa. A benefit of this reportage is the extent to which researchers are thus disabused of potential distortions, superficial conclusions, and theoretical explanations that can arise when thought occurs apart from lived habituation (since all persons possess biases, their own natural propensities are toward preconceived notions of ideal types). Further, this approach represents a Reformation emphasis: to take seriously the sacredness of everyday people amid ordinary life and vocation. Charles Taylor observes: "What is important for my purpose is this positive side, the affirmation that the fullness of Christian life was to be found within the activities of this life,

---

5. Robert Kolb, "Contemporary Lutheran Understandings of the Doctrine of Justification," in *Justification: What's at Stake in the Current Debates*, ed. Mark Husbands and Daniel J. Treier (Downers Grove, IL: InterVarsity, 2004), 159.

6. Jaroslav Pelikan, *The Vindication of Tradition* (New Haven: Yale University Press, 1984).

in one's calling and in marriage and the family. The entire modern development of the affirmation of ordinary life was, I believe, foreshadowed and initiated, in all its facets, in the spirituality of the Reformers."[7]

Lutheran churches and others in the rural developing world endure harsh climatic conditions, like severe droughts leading to famine, precluding sustainable levels of agricultural production for either personal consumption or transport to market. The immediacy and urgency of this food insecurity—exacerbated by economic and ecological factors—often places these communities on the brink of despair and death. That humans are able naturally and normally to conclude that their livelihoods ought to provide the possession and practice of avenues to exercise their agency to sustain their own lives, and that humans so readily surmise that these pathways and practices have by evil become treacherously interrupted, implies not only that the created order is, via natural law, intended for good and for justice, but that the whole cosmos (natural and human) yearns for righteousness with equity. The Christian solution to this quandary is Jesus Christ, the Word become flesh, whose incarnation follows concretely a path to culture in all of its manifestations, including agriculture and vocation. To spiritualize any doctrine—especially the hallmark Lutheran theology of justification by grace—renders it a metaphysical abstraction, segmenting it from faith lived *in concreto*, in real life. Joseph Sittler articulates this point: this "Word is not naked, it is historically embodied . . . and culture is the name for that ecological matrix in which the embodied will and deed from above addresses the embodied hearer at every point along history's river."[8]

A lesson for Western Christians from theologians in the developing world consists of the commensurability of justice and

7. Charles Taylor, *Sources of the Self* (Cambridge: Cambridge University Press, 1989), 218.

8. Joseph Sittler, *The Ecology of Faith* (Philadelphia: Muhlenberg, 1961), 5.

justification—they are not bifurcated, with justice as a precondition for justification ("no justice, no peace") or with justice as a resultant and distant fruit, disconnected from justification, as in an antinomian passivity that preserves the status quo. To know God's grace in Christ by faith or to be known by him is to be justified. It is also to know the justice of God meant for the world. Possession and practice are thereby conjoined: the possession of justification is tantamount to the practice of justice in the world. Theologians with postcolonial ears to hear press the West audibly with this reminder: "On the basis of our justification, we are not expected to consciously and deliberately perpetrate systemic or structural sin of any kind against God's creation. In this regard Luther remains relevant to Africa, a continent which has suffered much socio-political injustice."[9] Or, to cite Vítor Westhelle, who illustrates the same with this fresh translation of Luther: "Behold the new definition of justice (*definicion em novam iusticiae*): justice is the knowledge of Christ (*iusticia est cognitio Christi*)."[10] Thus, justice, interpreted theologically, cannot be reduced to political strategy or philosophical concept, or defined abstractly whether through idealization, idolatry, or fetishization. To know the justice God has fully accomplished in Christ's redemption is to know the person of Christ and his justification. Not to know Christ, not to work for God's justice in the world, is to be a sinner needing justification. The difficulty of this knowledge, and the necessity for repentance, is noted by Luther in the first of his 95 Theses: "When our Lord and Master Jesus Christ said, 'Repent' [Matt. 4:17], he willed the entire life of believers to be one of repentance."[11]

Noting a fatigue regarding the topic of justice—and with Chris-

9. Tom Joseph Omolo, "Luther in Africa," in *The Oxford Handbook of Martin Luther's Theology*, ed. Robert Kolb, Irene Dingel, and Ľubomír Batka (Oxford: Oxford University Press, 2014), 622.

10. Vítor Westhelle's translation from Martin Luther, *Lectures on Isaiah* (1527–30) (*LW* 17:225; *WA* 31/2:432–40).

11. *LW* 31:25.

tians engaging in talk about justice unmoored from justification—Miguel De La Torre in *Doing Christian Ethics from the Margins* declaims: "justice has become a worn-out, hollow expression—an abstract and detached battle cry. Every political action initiated by the dominant culture, no matter how self-serving, is construed as just."[12] This self-critical limitation and litmus informs the question posed to two individuals working for Lutheran, faith-based organizations in postcolonial settings and also intends to echo Luther's description of life prior to his experience of a gracious God: what is it that drives people in the African communities where you work "down to the deepest pit of despair"?

Evidentiary Testimonies

Linda Funke is a spouse and mother, who is best described as a missionary social worker—she holds a master's degree in social work and is, by professional church vocation, a deaconess in the Lutheran tradition. She is also certified as a teacher. She offers this reply to the question:

> I think what drives people on the African continent "down to the deepest pit of despair" is the same as what drives people to despair throughout the world—the loss of hope and dignity. If there were just one identifiable cause, we would have a lot easier time fixing it, but unfortunately it is often a conglomeration of

12. Miguel De La Torre, *Doing Christian Ethics from the Margins* (Maryknoll, NY: Orbis, 2004), 8. One problem in relation to justice has to do with those at opposite poles who either justify their actions in pursuit of innocence or seek blood in pursuit of vindication. Derek Walcott points to this as a fact of colonialism: "Who, in the depth of conscience, is not silently screaming for pardon or for revenge. The pulse of New World history is the racing pulse beat of fear, the tiring cycles of stupidity and greed." "The Muse of History," in *What the Twilight Says* (New York: Farrar, Straus and Giroux, 1998), 39.

many causes, including but not limited to corrupt governments and systems that leave people without a voice, a lack of community support, violence without resolution and healing, a lack of access to resources which would allow them the freedom to find their own solutions, and a lack of meaning in their lives.[13]

Evariste Karangwa is a spouse and father. He holds a doctor of philosophy in animal sciences degree from the University of Kentucky. Since 1991, he has worked in the international development field and serves as the senior director for Africa at Lutheran World Relief. He offers this reply to the question:

A response from an African woman: I'd be in the pit of despair because my children die of preventable diseases, I don't have property rights, I don't have rights to make decisions about family resources, and culturally, it's acceptable for my husband to beat me. If I'm from a conflict zone, rape is used as a weapon against me. International and national legal frameworks that either are absent or not enforced, lack of attention of programs to work with men to change attitudes (that sharing power and resources helps him and his family).[14]

Both the career development worker and the missionary—who have in common a vocation in Lutheran organizations and location of work in Africa but do not know one another—offer replies that redound with structural, exterior components: corrupt governments, unenforced rule of law, community dysfunction, violence, silencing apparatuses, abusiveness, rape, restriction of rights and access. None of this injustice could occur without tacit and active approval of structures: "We must always take sides. Neutrality helps

13. Response from Linda Funke via email correspondence, September 10, 2015.
14. Response from Evariste Karangwa via email correspondence, September 11, 2015.

the oppressor, never the victim. Silence encourages the tormentor, never the tormented."[15] As such, it is structures that influence negatively personal dignity, a group's sense of meaning, and its members' freedom to work their way out of situations of poverty. The force of these vicious vectors can be implicit but is no less tyrannical, mutually reinforcing, and destabilizing—so much so that the lines between natural and human disasters are blurred, and the distinction between slow and sudden-onset disasters becomes blended. Human behavior impacts and is impacted by environmental conditions in a manner that is turned cyclically in on itself.

Sin through a Postcolonial Lens

Structural sin functions, expectedly, in an exact opposite manner from God's salvation. Salvation breaks into this world both without equivocation and with externality, *extra nos*. As Luther notes:

> Let us thank God, therefore, that we have been delivered from this monster of uncertainty. . . . And this is the reason why our theology is certain: it snatches us away from ourselves and places us outside ourselves, so that we do not depend on our own strength, conscience, experience, person or works, but depend on that which is outside of ourselves, that is, on the promise and truth of God, which cannot deceive.[16]

Because of the inherently furtive and parasitic character of sin, it thrives preeminently when embedded within a host entity. For people living in the developing world, structural sin is often embedded

15. Elie Wiesel, acceptance speech, in *The Nobel Prizes 1986*, ed. Wilhelm Odelberg (Stockholm: Nobel Foundation, 1987). Accessed on-line on January 21, 2016 (http://www.nobelprize.org/nobel_prizes/peace/laureates/1986/wiesel-acceptance_en.html).

16. *Lectures on Galatians* (*LW* 26:387).

in colonialism. Thus, it may be helpful to look at the relationship between colonialism, postcolonialism, and structural sin. For the sake of clarity and scope, I provide these definitions:

> Colonialism represents a nationalistic ideology with a purportedly civilizing mission, often reinforced by a religious framework, legitimating the total or partial invasion and suzerainty of another's land and people—extending beyond geography to their relationships, souls, intellects, and imaginations—accruing usually to the occupier an economic and/or military advantage.

> Postcolonialism represents a critical and self-critical intervention of colonialism's invasionary proposals and practices to the extent that colonialist structures are destabilized and transformed and a transfigured identity is reclaimed, asserted, and recognized.[17]

The interventions of theologically grounded postcolonialism include a diagnosis of spiritual ailment and an invitation to a life of repentance, inhered in the notions of transformation and transfiguration. In a historical sense, sin takes on ecological implications in colonialism due to the willful compromise of suzerainty, the ravaging of "another's land and people," with a goal of economic advantage—this covetous expansionism is fueled by a fundamental

---

17. Paul Breslin's poem prepared for and recited at Derek Walcott's eightieth birthday presents a rhapsodic, versified, and image-rich representation of postcolonialism. The context for this poem was a gathering of Walcott scholars—whose works, themselves, arrive at no unanimity of definition for postcolonialism. "What is The Post-Colonial? we asked, like Pilate / keen for a rope or trope to bind up truth. / It is / an artificial heart, to which the branching arteries / of untranslated languages whose speakers are dying off, / histories three millennia long by a stone's-throw wide, / intricate rituals that morphed each mile along the trade-routes / have all been sutured, that they might converge / on a single chamber, to be spoken of by us / in languages whose speakers number billions" (unpublished recitation).

theological miscomprehension of the Creator's directive "to have dominion" (Genesis 1) with that Creator's intent for humans to be curators and caretakers of the creation. The historic complicity of the Christian church in colonialist expansion is regrettable and with contrition must be repented of in order for absolution to be received—for the church's own recovery of authority and integrity and for the transfiguration of economically disenfranchised and ecologically disfigured communities to find healing and redemption from their own haunting, historical legacies. "Missionaries of all kinds trumpeted the dynamic duo of 'Christianity and commerce.' Beginning with slavery, evangelicals had steadfastly claimed that free labor and commerce were a path to civilization."[18] The link between these three in Europe's embrace of its *mission civilisatrice* (civilizing mission)—Christianity, commerce, and colonialism—formed a key "trifecta for progress," constituting a rancid raveling of religion and economics with unprecedented exteriority. New technologies and new forms of transportation extended this legacy proficiently. A new habitation and innovative set of linkages for structural sin had been laid in the name of exploration, a new manifestation to carry an "ancient affliction," to employ the poet Derek Walcott's description.[19]

In the Lutheran tradition sin is radical (*radix*), its displacement penetrating; that is, not only at a personal level is it severe, but also the shrapnel of Eden's collapse leaves untouched no social situation, no ecological system, no natural network, no economic process, and no human structure—including the church to the extent that the church, like redeemed individuals, is itself *simul justus et peccator*. Simply put, from abortion to all of the abbreviations of life that happen due to poverty and racism, God's prophetic word issues forth with a seamless witness to life and full human flourishing;

18. Michael N. Barnett, *Empire of Humanity: A History of Humanitarianism* (Ithaca, NY: Cornell University Press, 2011), 67.

19. Derek Walcott, "Six Fictions," in *Bounty* (New York: Farrar, Straus and Giroux, 1998).

God's call addresses the complex systems that perpetuate the compromise of human persons. The gravity of sin extends beyond its common metaphors and analogies: brokenness, alienation, moral failure, fallenness, missing the mark—none of which have the effect of conveying the presence of the demonic or the utter absence of goodness implied in the level of turpitude inherent in biblical understandings of sin.

But this gravitas with which sin is taken in Lutheran theology complemented by the numerical success of Lutheran churches in the developing world affords this tradition a unique opportunity to couple structural sin with postcolonial analysis. The examination begins with liturgical doctrine, the poetics, the practice of faith (*fides quae creditur*). In the hymnal of the Lutheran Church–Missouri Synod (LCMS),[20] for example, confessions of sin include an admission before God and neighbor of "unworthiness," of being a "poor, miserable sinner," and of being "by nature sinful and unclean." Yet an equally important Lutheran contrast is that the grip of sin's hold and the depth of sin's cut, while pervasive and primordial, are not essential to what it means to be human. This matters because structural sin, even though it might infiltrate a system to a large extent, cannot become definitive of a group or community's identity. Not "They are racists," but "They are behaving in a racist manner" because "they," like "we," are not defined by their actions. As gravely as Lutherans take sin, that fault is not constitutive or ontological in Lutheranism.

The differences between two German theologians in the sixteenth century will help to elaborate this point. Matthias Flacius Illyricus (1520–75) was as ardently anti-freewill as he was zealously anti-Catholic. As contrasted with Philip Melanchthon's (1497–1560) more accommodating efforts, Flacius was such a rigorist that it earned him the legacy of a heterodox teaching named after him, Flacianism. His theological anthropology and his teachings on

20. *Lutheran Service Book* (St. Louis: Concordia, 2006).

42

original sin were rejected in the Lutheran Confessions[21] where, albeit caricatured, they came to be described as Manichaean. While Flacius, of course, did not himself propound Manichaeanism, there was a concern among his opponents that his theology could result in a comparable stridency with respect to human nature as essentially and autonomously evil.[22] The most odious implications of this teaching were with respect to the way the logic of Flacianism compromised the incarnation. While dead in sin, when humans are born again (*regeneratio*), they are made alive (*vivificatio*) in Christ, who necessarily took on fully human nature, yet without sin (Eph. 2:5).[23] Self-evidently, the sinful nature persists as long as we are in the flesh (Gal. 5:17).[24]

The Dignity of Life for All

The Lutheran definition from the *Formula of Concord* is clear. Despite original sin, God recognizes all human persons as his own work, created in his own image, designed for lives that give glory to him within the full field of creation. Christians, therefore, do not

21. "On the other hand, we also reject the false teaching of the Manichaeans, when it is taught that original sin is something essential and autonomous that Satan has infused into human nature and mixed together with it, as when poison and wine are mixed" (*BC*, Art. 1, Negative Theses 7).

22. "The non-Christian thinker Mani lent his name to a radical dualism which posited more or less equally powerful divine forces or persons on the side of good and the side of evil. Opponents of Flacius and his followers used the term 'Manichaean' to designate his view that original sin is the fallen human nature's essence in its 'formal' dimension, that is, in relationship to God. The term 'formal' was used in its Aristotelian sense of that which determines what a thing is as its design. The opponents' equation of his views with those of the ancient Manichaeans was based on their fear of where his views could lead, not on Flacius's actual teaching" (*BC*, 490, footnote).

23. *FC* III.

24. *FC* II:84.

resign themselves to a Manichaean fatalism or a "grin and bear it" worldview that is unable to envision any amelioration of human suffering. People possess Spirit-given agency, freeing them from the hegemony of structural sin's power and from the captivity to being oppressors, by nature, or to becoming perpetual victims in a defeated state of multigenerational dependency. Indeed, the poor we will always have with us, Jesus states (Matt. 26:11), but the persistence of poverty does not preclude or presume as futile those efforts to work on the elimination of suffering any more than the inevitability of car accidents does not preclude efforts to make automobile travel safer through technology, regulation, and education. On the contrary, Deuteronomy 15 infers that the presence of poverty provides precisely an opportunity to contribute something to those who suffer from it: "If anyone is poor among your fellow Israelites in any of the towns of the land the LORD your God is giving you, do not be hardhearted or tightfisted toward them. Rather, be open-handed and freely lend them whatever they need" (vv. 7–8). The suffering of people living in poverty should be seen as an invitation to action; those living lives of praise do deeds of love when they see a neighbor in need because they know the One from whom all blessings flow. Such a disposition of abundance, of overflow living, of life bursting with life, derives most actively from those who curate and care for the creation.

Contemporary Implications

Martin Luther King Jr., an heir to the German Reformer in more ways than the similarity of their names, called from "the dull monotony of a narrow jail cell" in Birmingham, Alabama, for a critique of the "contemporary church." Fifty years later the mainline, mainstream church remains, as it relates to dialogues about justice, "a weak, ineffectual voice with an uncertain sound. It is so often the arch-supporter of the status quo. Far from being disturbed by the presence of the church, the power structure of the average community is consoled by the church's silent sanction of things as they are."[25]

King, in the simplest of terms, is here aligning himself with Luther and Lutheran thought in multiple regards. First, sin is aided and abetted by dispositions of fatalism and quietism. It survives because there is no intervention. Second, justice depends on a positive approach to Christian ethics—namely, not only does justice require avoidance of evil, but, like sin, it is deeply embedded in systemic processes. Within these there must be the intentional pursuit of sin's corresponding opposite, the doing of good that is subversive of evil and promotional of evil's obverse—transforming and transfiguring, incrementally and instrumentally, the very structure itself. When people commit murder they kill, but people also kill when they do not defend life. As Luther's *Large Catechism* puts it, Christians are guilty "not only when we do evil, but also when we have the opportunity to do good . . . but fail to do so."[26] The Lutheran tradition does not endorse a view that only direct, personal action constitutes sin. For example, the seventh commandment addresses economic opportunism and structural sin: "Stealing is not just robbing someone's safe or pocketbook, but also taking advantage of someone in the market, in all stores and . . . wherever business is transacted and money is exchanged for goods and services."[27]

Martin Luther and Martin Luther King Jr. would agree that to not take action when there is an opportunity for good—especially if accompanied by a call of conscience—is at best seen as a tacit approval of injustice and at worst seen as a participation in structural sin. In the case of "beware how you deal with the poor,"[28] Luther assigns culpability, accountability, and responsibility to the people

25. Martin Luther King Jr. and James Melvin Washington, *A Testament of Hope: The Essential Writings and Speeches of Martin Luther King Jr.* (San Francisco: HarperSanFrancisco, 1991), 300.

26. Martin Luther, *Large Catechism* (*BC*, 412).

27. *BC*, 416–20.

28. *BC*, 419.

at the helm of systems, to the government and those in authority—even though identifying the precise culprit of evil is more difficult when the injustice is embedded with a system: "it is the responsibility of princes and magistrates . . . to establish and maintain order in all areas of trade and commerce in order that the poor may not be burdened and oppressed."[29] The political theorist Iris Marion Young puts it like this: "To judge a circumstance unjust implies that we understand it at least partly as humanly caused, and entails the claim that something should be done to rectify it. On the other hand, when the injustice is structural, there is no clear culprit to blame and therefore no agent clearly liable for rectification."[30] Luther acknowledges the difficulty of attributing liability. This is perhaps nowhere clearer than in today's debates over climate change and shifting weather patterns. What is clear, however, is who suffers the most from environmental degrading: the poorest of the poor, farmers in situations of encroaching desertification in places like the Sahel region of Africa.

Luther condemns the surreptitious, self-justifying, responsibility-avoiding, justice-averting "clever tricks and shrewd tactics"[31] among individuals who try "to accumulate as much as he or she can." These "rascals" (Luther's word) are "abetted by jurists and lawyers who twist and stretch the law to suit their purpose, straining words and using them for pretexts, without regard for equity or for our neighbor's plight." In short, whoever is "sharpest and shrewdest in such matters gets the most advantage out of the law." They give "the appearance of legality" as "they practice bribery through friendly connections" with "such lovely pretexts which the world does not consider wrong."[32]

In conclusion, the prophetic dimension already inherent in the

29. *BC*, 419.

30. Iris Marion Young and Danielle S. Allen, *Justice and the Politics of Difference* (Princeton: Princeton University Press, 2011), 95.

31. *BC*, 426.

32. *BC*, 427.

Lutheran tradition provides the material to address vividly a post-colonial context with a confessional theology of structural sin. God's Law addresses with critical and self-critical reflection the human condition through Luther's catechetical ethics. God's Law always accuses (*lex semper accusat*). This use of the Law remains anchored in the cornerstone Lutheran doctrine of justification by grace because it does not seek to drive the hearer "down to the deepest pit of despair," but toward the gospel and redemption that come from Jesus Christ, lived out in justice and in the care of creation.

CHAPTER 3

Simul Justus et Peccator

....

God's Mercy for a Culture of Violence and Death

In 2005, Norman Thomas published a provocative essay on the witness of the gospel in a post-9/11 world.[1] He reflected on how the problem of reconciliation versus new forms of violence is the most critical issue for the witness of the faith in a post-9/11 world. The United States is a vigilant country at "war against terrorism" since this tragic event. This is also the case with other nations at the receiving end of violence and destruction. This tragic event, however, has inflamed the mainstream North American spirit with an attitude of "us" against "them." It is also brewing within mainstream Anglo-Protestant culture in response to the ever-growing US Latino population. This belligerent attitude, in the words of the eminent Harvard professor Samuel Huntington, is fermenting a "major potential threat to the cultural and possible political integrity of the United States."[2] It is definitely hurting and hindering in many and various ways the witness of the gospel in North America. Our witness of the gospel in the twenty-first century must be reimagined in light of this fact. We must address and seek to dissipate our present

---

1. Norman E. Thomas, "Radical Mission in a Post-9/11 World: Creative Dissonances," *International Bulletin* (January 2005): 2–7.

2. Huntington, *Who Are We?* 51–53.

atmosphere of exclusion. The question is: how should we do this in light of our Reformation heritage and witness of the gospel?

Love of Enemy in Our Witness of the Gospel

Walter Wink in *Jesus and Nonviolence: A Third Way* proposes the place where we should begin in reimagining the witness of the gospel for our times. He writes:

> I submit that the ultimate question today is no longer the Reformation's "How can I find a gracious God?" It is instead, "How can I find God in my enemy?" What guilt was for Luther, the enemy has become for us: the goad that can drive us to God. What was formerly a purely private affair—justification by faith through grace—has now, in our age, grown to embrace the world. As John Stomer comments, we can no more save ourselves from sin, but God's amazing grace offers to save us from both. There is in fact no other way to God for our time but through our enemy, for loving the enemy has become the key, both to human survival in an age of terror and to personal transformation. Either we find the God who causes the sun to rise on the evil and on the good, or we may have no more sunrises.[3]

Note that Wink is not rejecting the problem of sin and guilt as part of the human condition and experience. He is also not rejecting the need for a personal relationship with God. However, he understands that the number one imperative for the witness of the Reformation gospel today is to embrace the world with God's love and mercy. The Catholic Church and the LWF forcefully underlined this point as

3. Walter Wink, *Jesus and Nonviolence: A Third Way* (Minneapolis: Fortress, 2003), 60.

one of their five critical imperatives to commemorate the Reformation: "Catholics and Lutherans should witness together to the mercy of God."[4] This should also be a critical imperative for all Christian churches in our present divided world. This witness of God's grace in the twenty-first century, as Wink observes and I concur, can no longer be just a private affair. It has to be specifically directed to the societies within which we live and exist. "Loving our enemy has become the key." But how do we love our enemy in our present world inflamed with hate and violence? Our Reformation heritage points to the unmasking of our sin as the first step in the process. The most crucial part is the unmasking of our idolatry.

The Unmasking of Idolatry

When Luther was teaching and writing on the Minor Prophets (1524–27), he was also reflecting on the problem of idolatry. During 1527–28 he wrote his *Large Catechism*, which was finally published in April 1529. It is in his explanation of the first commandment that we find his most cherished statement in defining and unmasking idolatry.[5] Luther understood that we create idols because of our human tendency to dominate, domesticate, and sacralize God in terms of our self-interest. Luther's unmasking of idolatry is best understood by taking a look at his lectures and commentaries on the Minor Prophets. Here we find that idolatry is a malady and sin that even a sacred society possesses because of self-interest. It is not just the problem of individual sinners. Luther calls in many texts and places in his commentaries on the Minor Prophets for the unmasking and rejection of this idolatry.

Luther's commentary on Amos is crucial in understanding his views on idolatry. He unmasks first of all the end result of idolatry

4. *FCTC*, 88.
5. *BC*, 86.

as he comments on Amos 2:4: "He [Amos] rebukes Judah, beginning with the source of all sins, namely, idolatry, which abandons the true worship and Word of God. After all, he struggled with this wickedness perpetually. You see, abominable idolatry necessarily follows when we depart from the true Word of God—something we see not only here but in all Scripture."[6] Idolatry is not only the root of all of our sins, but it is also the cause that distorts our true corporate worship of God. We need to understand, however, what Luther means when he states that "abominable idolatry necessarily follows when we depart from the true Word of God." Luther is not making reference here to a *corpus doctrinae* but rather to the domestication of the Word of God in order to serve the purposes and ambitions of the priests, prophets, and princes in power within the community.[7] Luther offers a succinct explanation of this critique in his comments on Amos 1:1. He explains here the prophetic ministry of Amos in sharp contrast to the "prophets, priests, and wise men," who according to the right order and pedigree of the times, were in charge of the "ministry of the Word." "Whatever they would establish or teach the people would accept as most sacred."

However, Luther observes that these legitimate figures became "puffed up," authenticating their idolatrous actions and behaviors as the norm and established truths within Scripture. However, Amos was a shepherd from Tekoa. It is out of the mouth of this simple, marginalized shepherd, who lived within the reality of the people of

---

6. Martin Luther, *Minor Prophets I: Hosea–Malachi* (LW 18:138–39).

7. In reading and translating Luther's commentaries on Hosea, Amos, Joel, Haggai, and Jonah from his Latin lectures, I have found Luther using the term *verbum Dei* to indicate the Word of God as the verb or active word of God incarnate. In other contexts the term *verbum Dei* clearly refers to the text of the Word of God. In some contexts when Luther makes reference to the *verbum Dei* as the active Verb of God he is pointing out that this Word cannot be domesticated to serve the idols of power. There is a clear example of this dynamics in the preface to Amos (*WA* 13:159). The sustenance of our bodies is in Luther's interpretation the *verbum dei*, which is unfortunately translated in the English rendition as the "Word of God" (*LW* 18:127).

God, that God speaks. Luther also observes how it is God's custom
to do this throughout history:

> In contempt of those who became so proud, the Lord, however,
> often aroused humble, common people who belonged to nei-
> ther the prophetic nor priestly order. These lowly people thus
> would resist all those others; they would rebuke them for their
> wickedness, as we can see here and there in the prophets. This,
> however, is the "folly" of God, by which He makes foolish the
> world and the wisdom of the flesh (cf. I Cor. 1:20f.). These were
> very lowly,[8] very humble people. It seemed insane for them to
> want to resist kings and so many prophets and priests, who
> were in charge of the ministry of the Word, as well as a prudent
> people taught in the Law of the Lord. It seemed insane for such
> men to want to teach something new and outside of the normal
> custom. These humble men, therefore, were considered fools.[9]

In other words, the right Word, the norm from God, can become a
tool of idolatry at any given time. Luther is keenly aware also, as he
interprets Amos 2:5, that this most sacred reading, the reading of
what is considered the "true Word of God" by the accepted dominant interpreters, is also perpetuated from parents to children.[10]
This is why God raises throughout the various times in history
prophets who arise from the margins. They are the lowliest and
humblest among the people.[11] They are attuned to the daily lives

8. I chose the translation "the most marginalized" because Luther uses here
abiectissimi in Latin (*WA* 18:161).

9. *LW* 18:129. Luther finds during his times the office of the papacy establishing
the idolatrous normalcy of the Word. He offers, however, in interpreting Amos an
understanding of how idolatry corrupts the sacred and God's revelation in history.

10. *LW* 18:139; *WA* 13:167.

11. See Orlando E. Espín, *Idol and Grace: On Traditioning and Subversive Hope*
(Maryknoll, NY: Orbis, 2014), 20–21. Espín makes a bold and accurate claim how
the Word of God has been written, interpreted, and proclaimed in the New Testament not by the educated elite but rather by the less "educated." In fact, God's

and needs of the community, and speak the liberating Word of God to the ones in power and to the most dejected. These prophets shatter the idols of power and transform the present as they speak "something new and outside of the normal custom."[12]

The question at stake is: what kind of idolatrous behavior is being inflicted by the "stewards" of the faith, as they proclaim the Word among the people? Luther pinpoints many and various ways in which these idolatrous stewards "twist or pervert" the daily lives and personal affairs of the afflicted in Amos 2:6-12.[13] Father and son abuse and rape the most vulnerable women, their maids, who labor in their homes. They acquire wrongly their goods from the poor, fine the poor, and extort them, "to live in luxury and to indulge in their appetite very freely." Luther observes that what is most damaging is not that they live in luxury but that they do so by obtaining their material goods unfairly from the poor through their acquired powers from the sacred. Luther poignantly underscores that this practice occurs at the center of the temple's community and life (in what we call in Spanish their *convivir*) and it is in this manner that they inflict the greatest blasphemy and profanation of God's temple.[14] Luther accentuates this way of life and worship as the most injurious and damaging idolatry in the life of God's chosen people. This is how he comments in reference to Amos 3:9:

> 9. *Proclaim to the strongholds in Ashdod.* He is comparing the surrounding nations with the people of God so that the latter may become confounded and ashamed of their own wickedness when they see that they surpass even the heathen. It is as if the prophet were saying: "Look, you heathen who live around

---

proclamation has become powerful and evident "among the majority of Christians, throughout most of Christian history, [who] have been illiterate" (20).

12. Luther reiterates this point in his interpretation of Joel 2:28 (*LW* 18:106; *WA* 13:100).

13. *LW* 18:140–43; *WA* 13:167–71.

14. *LW* 18:140–41; *WA* 13:167.

us! Gather to us. Make a test whether we can be compared with you. The people who want to be called God's people surpass in wickedness you who do not worship the true God." This is how nearly all the prophets almost justify the heathen in a comparison with wicked Israel. Ezekiel writes this way in chapter 16:48: "Your sister Sodom and her daughters have not done as you and your daughters have done."[15]

The worst kind of idolatry is not the one of worshiping a different god instead of the biblical God. It is not about missing the mark concerning right belief and doctrine. In fact, God honors the "heathen" over against those sacred privileged ones, when the chosen ones dishonor and blaspheme God's sacred space by inflicting pain in this *convivir* (the everyday sharing of life and community) of the most marginalized and the poor in their midst.

Overcoming Idolatry in Proclaiming
the Mercy of God in North America

We must be cognizant of our structural sin. Individuals or groups of people are not kept at the margins by one individual or a couple of individuals acting on their own account. It is a malady that affects how we act as a people within a society. It is a sin that attacks and invades all Christian churches and societies. When we hate a group of people and call them "our enemies" or when we simply keep them at an arm's length to exclude them within our society, we are engaging in an idolatrous position of power. This is taking place today with great intensity in North American society. This human condition is not, however, the exclusive sin and malady of "Anglo" culture and churches. All cultures and civilizations fall prey to this human hunger for power and exclusion of the other. This is also

15. *LW* 18:147; *WA* 13:173.

part of the equation. This chapter will not ignore this global reality. E. M. Coiran in his classic work *A Short History of Decay* poignantly reminds us of this fact: "The great persecutors are often recruited from the martyrs not quite beheaded."[16] However, this realization does not excuse us from seeing how this plays out in contemporary North American culture. We find as a sign of the times a growing hatred and exclusion of Hispanic and Latino communities in the United States. This is also an attitude among many Christian churches in North America. How have we arrived at this juncture and what can Christian churches do to overcome this atmosphere of exclusion? This is central to our reimagining of the witness of God's mercy for today.

All countries have a mainstream, or core, culture. In terms of the United States it has been the Anglo-Protestant culture that has been the backbone in the shaping of the North American identity. It has also been the backbone in the founding and shaping of political and social institutions in North America for the past four hundred years.[17] There are many valuable core values that we have inherited from this "dissenting Protestant culture" in North America.[18] At the same time, we have also suffered many injurious things from the idolatrous behavior present within this culture. All cultures offer hints of the presence of God in creation but at the same time they take at times the forms of idolatrous expressions of the sacred. This is the present paradox of our human condition. We have seen above how Luther and the Minor Prophets were

16. E. M. Coiran, *A Short History of Decay*, trans. Richard Howard (London: Quartet Book, 1990), 4.

17. Huntington, *Who Are We?* 59–106.

18. Huntington, *Who Are We?* 67–72. I find among the most valuable core values (mostly de jure but not always de facto) the affirmation of the dignity of the individual human being, the fundamental equality of all human beings, the "inalienable rights of life, liberty, and the pursuit of happiness." I believe, however, that the "American ideal" that we are all playing on an even playing field, and the notion that everyone can achieve greatness if they try hard enough, is simply a myth and an illusion that sidetracks our understanding of inequality.

cognizant of this fact. How has this idolatrous behavior come to be in North America?

In spite of the so-called separation of church and state in the United States, we have a civil religion. There are two foundational elements of our civil religion. First, we are the nation that primarily trusts God among all nations and we are blessed by this fact. Second, the United States is a chosen nation, the one nation with a special destiny under God, the new Israel.[19] Our laws, our way of life, are far above the grade. This is the generally accepted belief. I do not question that a nation may invoke God. What I do question is how our civil religion has been elevated to the level of the most sacred by many Christian church leaders and citizens in North America. This is not an exclusive malady of the United States. There are many nations whose form of government or political leadership has been elevated to the level of the sacred. They can do no wrong. In their opinion, the kingdom of God is truly present or manifested absolutely in their civil religion. This is also the case among several nations that have in their political and social agendas "a preferential option for the poor." There is, nevertheless, persecution of the people at the margins. The crucial problem for Christians in this age of exclusion is, therefore, how our civil religions become an absolute expression of the sacred. This is idolatry. This ideology has been appropriated by several North American churches as a bona fide doctrinal stand for Christianity. What is at stake?

For generations most immigrants who came to the United States adjusted to this way of life and bowed to the "American" identity and creed. This is no longer the case. Since the mid-twentieth century, North America has become an ever-growing multiethnic and multiracial society. The North American Anglo-Saxon way of life has been particularly challenged by the ever-growing

19. Huntington, *Who Are We?* 103–6. Huntington pinpoints the irony of this civil religion and American Creed: "While the American Creed is Protestantism without God, the American religion is Christianity without Christ" (106).

and predominant Hispanization of North America.[20] In the words of Samuel Huntington: "Mexican immigration is leading toward the demographic *reconquista* of areas Americans took by force in the 1830's and 1840's."[21] But they are not alone. Other Latinos have made their way into the United States due to previous policies of expansionism and political actions in Central America, the Caribbean, and South America by the US government. This overflowing of Latin waters into North America is perceived today as an inundation of the "American" identity. It has produced, therefore, a crisis in the "American" identity.

A new shaping of life and consciousness is taking place in the North American identity that cannot be stopped. However, this situation has accentuated a belligerent spirit of "us" (citizens) against "them" (immigrants). Hatred has been elevated to the level of the sacred and, to add insult to injury, in the spirit of national security. Latinos have made a great contribution to the United States, but now the North American predominant focus is to make scapegoats of these Latino immigrants. Strenuous laws have been passed in such states as Arizona against undocumented immigrants. Also, racial profiling and harassment are part of the order of the day. During the writing of this chapter, I received, for example, a note from a bona fide documented Mexican merchant in Milwaukee. She had received a threatening letter directing her to close her shop and move back to Mexico.

This atmosphere has made its way into the witness and life of many Protestant leaders and churches. In its extreme form we find Robert Jeffress, a prominent megachurch pastor from Dallas, making such hurtful statements as "Jesus wouldn't protect undocumented immigrants." The reason behind this is that the undocumented are characterized as "criminals" and, therefore, we should show no "mercy" to them. I could cite even more moderate

---

20. Huntington, *Who Are We?* 221–56.
21. Huntington, *Who Are We?* 221.

church leaders portraying this outlook. In fact, some said to me that no Christian pastor should be offering undocumented immigrants rides to church. The witness of God's love and mercy is completely absent from this "witness of the gospel." In many and various forms, I have found this spirit among US Christian leaders. "We" Christians dictate the order of the day to "them" because somehow "they" are not "Christians." This is the case because they are "delinquents" and as delinquents they should be excluded from our community of faith. It is in this posture that American civil religion has become an idolatrous *corpus doctrinae* in the life and practice of many North American churches and leaders. This is idolatry at its worst.

Our current postures of idolatry have also caused many "law-abiding citizens," including members of Christian churches, to take advantage of undocumented immigrants. They do so by paying them a miserable wage or no wage at all after they have performed skillful and needful tasks for their patrons. I have intervened in my role as a parish pastor in situations where undocumented women have worked as domestic servants, only to be treated with cruelty by their patrons with the threat of deportation dangling over their heads. I am aware of many Latinos who have fulfilled the "American Dream" in North America and have joined the ranks of oppressors against our less fortunate sisters and brother in the diaspora. This chapter is not written, however, to offer a political solution to a political problem.[22] It is about shattering and overcoming our idolatry for our times in light of our reimagining of the Reformation gospel. God's unquestionable mercy must resound in our society's ever-growing exclusion of the other. Wink's exhortation continues to resonate in my ears: "Either

22. I do not mean here that Christians are exempted from a public theology. Here I use "political" to point out that it is not the role of the church to provide a partisan political agenda to gain influence and power over others. The role of the church is precarious because the church must offer God's judgment as well as God's mercy to all.

we find the God who causes the sun to rise on the evil and on the good, or we may have no more sunrises."[23]

I have already taken the first step in showing how Luther rejected idolatry in his proclamation of the gospel. Groups of people, churches, may be engaging in idolatrous worship and an idolatrous way of life, even if they invoke "the true worship and Word of God."[24] Luther understood quite clearly how this idolatrous behavior plays out in light of the prophet Amos. This occurs when those in power show no mercy toward the needy and the poor. It also occurs when the stewards of the faith "twist or pervert" the daily lives and personal affairs of the afflicted for personal gain and glory.[25] This is a judgment that Luther proclaims loudly and clearly not against the sin of one person but against the idolatrous behavior of religious communities and societies. The proclamation that we are and can be totally sinful as a people must be applied here as we proclaim God's Law in our church and society. But this proclamation must also affirm above all how God's love and mercy overpower our idolatrous way of life. The unmasking of our idols must accompany our proclamation of God's concrete mercy for the enemy.

Reimagining the Reformation Witness of the Gospel

The Reformation witness has been shaped during the past five hundred years under the themes of *sola gratia, sola fide, sola scriptura,* and *solus Christus.* I am not rejecting these four wonderful themes of the Reformation. However, they need to be intensely reimagined in the realization that the God of life is the God of love and mercy. It would be helpful, in light of this perspective, to add another *sola* for the witness of the faith in the twenty-first century: *sola caritate*

---

23. Wink, *Jesus and Nonviolence*, 60.
24. *LW* 18:138–39.
25. *LW* 18:140–43; *WA* 13:167–71.

Dei. (*Caritas* is the usual Latin translation of *agapē.*) It is in this *sola* that we find God's ever-flowing mercy. This is our point of departure as we embrace the margins to give witness to the gospel. How do we connect these themes?

In 1 John 4, the key theme that predominates is our love of neighbor grounded in God's love. John tells us: "Everyone who loves has been born of God and knows God" (v. 7). The love that is distinguished here is God's unmerited, unconditional love, his *agapē* love. A popular text used in the witness of evangelical Christians is John 3:16: "For God so loved the world that he gave his only Son, so that everyone who believes in him may not perish but may have eternal life." Many have used this text to highlight that all that we need in life is to believe in Jesus Christ. It has also been used to show that the important thing in our lives is to have a personal relationship with Jesus Christ. But if we read "born of water and the spirit in order to enter the kingdom of God" (John 3:5) in the context of 1 John 4:7–21, this birth carries a concrete action in living God's love. We are called to live and exercise God's unconditional love for our neighbor. "We love God because he first loved us. If anyone says, 'I love God' yet hates his brother, he is a liar. For he who does not love his brother whom he has seen, cannot love God, whom he has not seen" (1 John 4:19–20).

First John affirms above all the active presence of God's *agapē* as the mark of our faith. In 1 John 3:11–15, this is explained in terms of concrete acts of love over hate. The key example offered by John in this case is the narrative concerning Cain and Abel (Genesis 4). We may say that the language of *sola gratia* and *sola fide* is demonstrated and affirmed in 1 John through the concrete action of God's love and mercy for the enemy and the stranger. The words proclaimed here by John are congruent, I believe, with the Sermon on the Mount. In Matthew, those who live God's concrete act of righteousness will be persecuted (Matt. 5:10). Those who live like Abel, in concrete acts of God's righteousness, which are, according to John (1 John 3:11–17), concrete actions grounded in God's love, should not be surprised "if the world hates you" (v. 13).

Luther was fond of the Gospel of John. He realized a lifelong dream in 1537, when he was able to spend a whole year preaching every Saturday in Wittenberg on the Gospel of John.[26] Luther was deeply influenced by John's proclamation of God's incarnate love early in his career. This is clearly expressed in Luther's explanation of his Heidelberg Theses (1518). Thesis 28 breathes in and out the centrality of the love of God incarnate expressed in 1 John 3. It is crucial for the witness of our faith. The thesis reads: "The love of God does not find, but creates that which is pleasing to it. The love of man comes into being through that which is pleasing to him." Luther explains what this means for the witness of the gospel:

> The first part is clear because the love of God which lives in man loves sinners, evil persons, fools, and weaklings in order to make them wise, righteous, and strong. Rather than seeking its own good the love of God flows forth. Therefore sinners are lovely because they are loved, they are not loved because they are lovely. For this reason the love of man avoids sinners and evil persons. . . . This is the love of the cross, born of the cross, which turns in the direction where it does not find good which it may enjoy but where it confers good upon the bad and needy person. . . . "Blessed is he who considers the poor," for the intellect cannot comprehend an object that does not exist, that is, the poor and needy person, but only a thing which does exist, that is, the true and good.[27]

26. See Martin Luther, *Sermons on the Gospel of St. John*, chapters 1–4 (*LW* 22:ix). During this time Luther was gravely ill for two months, almost to the point of death. The rest of these sermons are available in *LW*, vols. 23 and 24. Luther was the substitute preacher for Johannes Bugenhagen, who was ministering in Denmark in 1537.

27. Martin Luther, Heidelberg Disputation (*LW* 31:57). My revised translation of the English text.

I have been deeply impacted by this explanation since my early days in pastoral ministry. The very essence and witness of our Christian faith is grounded in the offer of God's incarnate love. This is really also an expression of God's own being and action. It is here where God's mercy is profoundly outpoured. The Christian church cannot give a witness to the faith by drawing a line between "us" and "them." People at the margins are to be loved unconditionally because God is and offers his unconditional love to all humanity. There cannot be a *sola fide, sola gratia,* without a *sola caritate Dei!* All people are mirrored in God's sight to become his chosen nation, his holy people, and to receive his mercy where there is no mercy (1 Peter 2:9-10). This is why God loves powerfully the people at the margins. God "confers good upon the bad and needy person." This is the kind of love that is grounded not in a mere intellectual affirmation of the faith. It is grounded in a living outpouring of God's love.[28] It is in God's concrete gift of himself where the "others" are acknowledged and restored as worthy human beings.[29] How do we live and proclaim this powerful offer of God's mercy in our present world?

---

28. Luther is very clear in his explanation of Thesis 28 that "it is the love of the cross, born of the cross" (*LW* 31:57). It is faith born, defined, and grounded in God's gift of his love. Luther and I are critical of Thomas Aquinas's understanding of Christian faith as *fides caritate formata,* if faith is the result of our human charity (works). However, Wolfhart Pannenberg observes: "Aquinas with his formula *fides caritate formata* was thinking of love of God as the motive for faith, and in another connection Luther, too, could uphold a close link between faith and love in the relation to God, especially when dealing with faith as a fulfilling of the first commandment" (Wolfhart Pannenberg, *Systematic Theology* [Grand Rapids: Eerdmans, 1991-98], 3:190). I would say that for Luther this is a crucial connection as explained above.

29. Tuomo Mannermaa (1937-2015), who is considered the father of the New Finnish Luther Research project, also accentuates God's love as the key to understanding Luther's entire theology. Mannermaa begins, where I also begin, in recognizing the centrality of the theology of the cross in Luther's Heidelberg Theses (1518). See Tuomo Mannermaa, *Two Kinds of Love: Martin Luther's Religious World,* trans. and ed. Kirsi I. Stjerna (Minneapolis: Fortress, 2010), 4. However, his approach is not focused on how God's incarnate love listens to the margins.

Living and Proclaiming the Mercy of God

First and foremost we must listen to the cry of the people at the margins. It is here that we are able to confront and unmask our sinful idolatrous beliefs and practices. But there must also be an outpouring of God's mercy and love among those who are marginalized. It is here where the Spirit of God dwells mightily. Luther expresses this in a powerful manner in his commentary on *The Magnificat*:

> Therefore to God alone belongs that sort of seeing that looks into the depths with their need and misery, and is near to all that are in the depths; as St. Peter says (1 Peter 5:5): "God opposes the proud but gives grace to the humble." And this is the source of men's love and praise of God. For no one can praise God without first loving Him. No one can love Him unless He makes Himself known to him in the most lovable and intimate fashion. And He can make Himself known only through those works of His which He reveals in us, and which we feel and experience within ourselves.[30]

Luther believes God does not abandon his people to the wretchedness of their idolatry. God unmasks and cuts through our idolatry in order to unfold his mercy and love: "God has imposed death on us all and laid the cross of Christ with countless sufferings and afflictions upon his beloved children."[31] God's purpose is to unmask and cut through "the world with its proud eyes" that "constantly thwarts God's presence and action in Jesus Christ."[32] This is done in order that the whole world might live in the transforming presence of God's love. According to Luther, this is what Mary's Song is all about: "The tender mother of Christ does the same here and teaches

30. *LW* 21:300.
31. *LW* 21:301.
32. *LW* 21:301.

us, with her words and by the example of her experience, how to know, love, and praise God."[33] However, the call is not merely to unmask idolatry. God also calls us to transform our idolatrous situations through his mercy. This is the second crucial step. The question is: how do we do this in our present age? The Sermon on the Mount offers concrete ways in which we can unmask our idolatry and proclaim God's mercy in a divided world.

The Sermon on the Mount and God's Mercy at the Margins

The key text for our consideration in the Sermon on the Mount is Matthew 5:38–47 (and the parallel text found in Luke 6:27–36). The Sermon on the Mount offers to followers of Jesus a programmatic way of life. Jesus is preparing his disciples to give a concrete witness of his mercy and love in the midst of the hatred that is directed toward them. This concrete exercise of God's mercy is offered at the same time that the idolatrous behavior of their enemies is being unmasked. The goal in this section is to break down the walls between "us" and "them" in the proclamation and acting out of God's mercy and love.

We have already noted how Luther was deeply influenced early in his career by John's proclamation of God's incarnate love.[34] For John the Apostle, a life lived in God's love is equivalent to living a life of faith. Luther captures this important teaching in John. For Luther, the proclamation of the gospel must underscore the sine qua

33. *LW* 21:301.

34. See note 28. Luther also preached regularly on the Gospel of Matthew during the absence of Bugenhagen from Wittenberg. He preached on Matthew 5–7 ca. 1530–32. Matthew was for Luther "an excellent evangelist for the instruction of the congregation, [who] records the fine Sermon of Christ on the Mount, and strongly urges the exercise of love and good works" (*LW* 53:68). At the same time he reaffirms in his preaching of Matthew 5:38–47 during this period that "he [Jesus] is speaking at the same time against the opinion of those pious people who hoped for the establishment through the Gospel of a new political order in opposition to the one they had previously accepted" (*LW* 67:33).

non of *sola gratia* as expressed by Paul in his epistles. However, the word "grace" is not used in the Gospels of Matthew and Mark. The Gospel of Luke uses the word "grace" four times (1:30; 2:40; 2:52; 4:22). In Luke 1:30 we find Mary being bestowed with God's gift of grace. Luke 2:40 and 2:52 are statements concerning Jesus shining forth God's gift of grace. Luke 4:22 is significant in that the crowds were amazed at Jesus's "gracious words." This statement is made in reference to Jesus's first sermon in the synagogue concerning his messianic work under the Spirit to bring new life to the vulnerable people of God. The most significant text in this context is Jesus's words offered in the Sermon on the Mount in Luke 6:27–32. Here Jesus challenges his disciples and his people "to love your enemies, do good to those who hate you" (v. 27).

Jesus's challenge and exhortation goes hand in hand with Wink's exhortation above. Jesus asks his disciples: "If you love those who love you, what credit is that to you?" Several other translations, including Spanish, use the word "merit" in place of "credit." I find this text quite provoking in the original Greek. My sense is that the original Greek may be read the following way: "If you love those who love you, what [kind of] mercy [grace] is this to you [*poia hymin charis estin*]?"[35] I realize that this is not the traditional translation of this verse. Nevertheless, it fits the context in which Jesus is questioning the disciples and also the primary meaning of *charis* (grace). God's gracious offer can be had only when God's unconditional gift of love is present for the stranger, even the enemy. Matthew offers this same emphasis even though he does not use the noun "grace" in Matthew 5:46.[36] What Luke and Matthew offer in

35. See J. P. Louw and Eugene A. Nida, *Greek-English Lexicon of the New Testament: Based on Semantic Domains*, 2nd ed. (New York: United Bible Societies, 1996), 1:748–49. The use of *charis* in this context, I believe, points to the showing of kindness with the implication of graciousness. This is the gift of God's unconditional love.

36. It reads: "For if you love those who love you, what reward [*misthos*] do you have?" *Misthos* signifies wages or recompense.

this text is the action on the part of the disciples, their witness of God's mercy and grace, and not what they receive for their actions. Gratuitousness is found in this offer of faith. This is the point.

This goes hand in hand with the text in Matthew 5:38–41:

> You have heard that it was said, "An eye for an eye and a tooth for a tooth." But I say to you, do not resist an evildoer. But if anyone strikes you on the right cheek, turn the other also; and if anyone wants to sue you and take your coat, give your cloak as well; and if anyone forces you to go one mile, go also the second mile.

How is the dialectic of Law and gospel present here? How are the dimensions of *simul justus et peccator* (totally sinful and totally justified) offered in the words of Jesus? Wink offers some important insights in light of the culture and society during Jesus's ministry that enlighten this reading.[37] His focus, however, is more grounded in a moral initiative to find a creative alternative to violence in a life of civil disobedience. My focus is on the Reformation gospel. It is grounded in disarming idolatry (personal and structural sin) while offering human and social transformation through God's love and mercy.

For Luther, the three examples cited above are grounded in Jesus's imperative "do not resist an evildoer." This is what guides his interpretation of this text.[38] Luther was uneasy at the time because he detected God's spiritual authority being confused with temporal human authority. He was particularly uneasy about how this posture resulted in the Peasants' Revolt (1525). This revolt was inspired by the Radical Reformation movement of Thomas Müntzer.[39] This movement promoted a violent revolution against those who got in the way of the Spirit. Luther accentuates, therefore, the distinction

37. Wink, *Jesus and Nonviolence*, 5–25.
38. *LW* 21:106.
39. *LW* 21:107.

between the two kingdoms. He finds this distinction and teaching in Jesus's Sermon on the Mount. Jesus is teaching his disciples the kind of people they should be.[40] In this posture, the Christian life can be exercised only through pure passivity and acceptance of the enemy. Luther finds, therefore, that Jesus directs his disciples in this reading to engage in pure passivity. This is not the case in another of Luther's writings prior to 1525.[41] But Luther observes in his commentary on the Sermon on the Mount that Jesus urges us to love in silence and not attempt to correct the situation. The role of correcting this set of affairs belongs to the government and not Christianity. Civil law should take care of violence and not Christians or Christian churches. I believe that Luther is correct in teaching that Christians or Christian churches should not take the law into their own hands. However, the Sermon on the Mount calls for Christians and Christian churches to engage in an active unmasking of idolatry in order to point to the transformative power of God's love and mercy. How is this done?

First, the imperative "do not resist an evildoer" is not a command to submit to evil or to be silent in the presence of evil and idolatry. The follower of Jesus is not to be hostile, not to engage in a violent rebellion.[42] The call, therefore, is not to engage in revenge or repay evil with evil. Luther understands this. However, he does

---

40. *LW* 21:105. The editor makes the following comment on this page: "This is one of the most explicit statements of the polemic underlying most of this commentary."

41. See Bayer, *Martin Luther's Theology*, 316–17. Bayer points out that Luther in his essay *Temporal Authority: To What Extent It Should Be Obeyed*, published in 1522 (*LW* 45:104; *WA* 11:261.26–27), affirms the right of passive resistance as a form of public protest. This is not clearly evident in his commentary on Jesus's Sermon on the Mount. Notice that Luther's essay on temporal authority was published before the Peasants' War (1525).

42. Wink, *Jesus and Nonviolence*, 10. The verb *anthistēmi* signifies "to oppose, to be hostile toward, to show hostility." See Louw and Nida, *Greek-English Lexicon of the New Testament*, 1:491. A number of Greek lexicons are consistent in showing how this verb signals an open hostile opposition to the enemy. This hostile action is what must be resisted.

not understand that this is not a call to be silent or passive. In fact, we find in reading the Gospels that Jesus was committed to the opposition of evil.[43] He was not silent concerning evil and idolatry. But Jesus's method was different from the one employed by the anti-Roman fighters during the time of his ministry. Evil was not fought with evil. Evil was confronted in the power of his mercy and love. Second, this way of mercy will be clearly understood if we take time to hear Jesus's sermon in its original social context.

The three examples used by Jesus—turning the other cheek, giving our cloak as well as our coat, and walking a second mile— illustrate Jesus's powerful message of disarming and calling for change within the sinful structures of the times. These illustrations are offered to bring into light and to disarm what dehumanizes people. Followers of Jesus are called in the same breath to transform those structures. This is done when people are considered with dignity and love in their marginality. I would like to offer as a case study Jesus's second example for the sake of brevity.

The second example is set in a court of law. It has to do with when someone is suing for a person's outer garment. Deuteronomy 24:10–17 offers guidance in cases like this. The situation was familiar to Jesus's listeners. Indebtedness was one of the most serious problems in first-century Palestine. The situation had to do with Roman policy and not natural calamity. Jesus's audience did not appreciate the system of their day. This was a system that subjected people in need to humiliation by stripping them of their lands, their goods, and even their inner garments. Why does Jesus counsel them to give over even their cloaks and their inner garments as well in the court of law? What would have been the result? The person suing

43. Luther notes that this is what Jesus does when he appears before Caiaphas (John 18:22–23). Jesus in fact declares his innocence and rebukes the high priest. However, Luther does not understand that for the Christian not seeking revenge does not mean being silent or passive. This is not how Luther reads turning the other cheek. Jesus is not calling Christians to be silent or passive in this text (cf. *LW* 21:106–7, and Wink, *Jesus and Nonviolence*, 13–15).

would be left in embarrassment with a coat in one hand and a cloak in the other hand. Why? Because the debtor sued would have been completely naked as a result of his action.

Nakedness was a taboo in Judaism (Gen. 9:20–27). Shame fell not only on the naked person but also on the person viewing or causing the nakedness. The religious system of the day prohibited this action for it valued the dignity and humanity of people in their community. Deuteronomy 24:17–18 offers the following punch line: "You shall not deprive a resident alien or an orphan of justice; you shall not take a widow's garment in pledge. Remember that you were a slave in Egypt and the LORD your God redeemed you from there; therefore I command you to do this." The Israelites had established the law not to take the garments of the poor. They could not leave the poor naked. Their dignity had to be preserved. The Israelites were to remember their oppression. They were also to remember how God had led them out of those oppressive structures because God heard their cries and was merciful to them.

Jesus calls his disciples and the people of God's kingdom to be especially merciful to those who live in the margins. This is done by unmasking the power of idolatry. It is done when those systems that go against the love and mercy of God are humiliated. In this humiliation Jesus points out how ridiculous and unloving are those systems and idols of power. Jesus not only unmasks those systems and the people who live under those idolatrous conditions but also calls them to see how merciful God is. This is what God offers in his transforming love and mercy. This witness, this gospel, is God's unconditional and transforming offer to those who build the wall of "us" against "them." This call is a call to bring down this wall of exclusion and hatred. It is a call to embrace all people in the mercy of God. In this call and action of God, we are no longer foreigners and aliens but fellow citizens with God's people (Eph. 2:14–21). The Sermon on the Mount in the context of Jesus's day empowers our reimagination of the Reformation witness of God's mercy for our time and place.

CHAPTER 4

Martyria and Mission

The Witness of Creative Disruption

Ambassadors for Christ are those through whom God is appealing to people to be reconciled by the gospel's message of reconciliation (2 Cor. 5:20). On occasion, they must engage others wisely in creative disruption that often appears to be non-reconciliatory. This chapter proposes a definition of creative disruption, the conditions and manner in which it is to occur, and the constructive benefits to God's kingdom of disruptive work.

To be evocative of Jaroslav Pelikan, creative disruption functions best when it is *creative*, with respect to tradition (furthering the living faith of deceased believers) and *disruptive* with respect to traditionalism (challenging the dead faith of those who are alive).[1]

Theological support for this idea will be interwoven throughout this chapter as well as historical considerations and general practical descriptions. This missiological consideration of creative disruption is predicated on a theological underpinning that, as Robert Kolb summarizes, joins with those who have "striven to demonstrate that Luther's proclamation of the God who justifies is not trapped inside sixteenth-century thought forms but is relevant and applicable to

---

1. Pelikan, *The Vindication of Tradition.*

the dilemmas and distresses of the twenty-first century."[2] In that sense, creative disruption is not an avant-garde breakthrough for missional leaders, but rather a reiteration of ancient truth revealed in the living tradition of Scripture alone (*sola Scriptura*) in a manner that constructively confronts the wounding captivity of traditionalism. Against this, the Spirit persists in witness with the ever-vivifying, ever-innovating doing of God's promises to God's people: "I am about to do a new thing; now it springs forth, do you not perceive it? I will make a way in the wilderness and rivers in the desert" (Isa. 43:19). As such, living traditions in which the Spirit's enkindling presence abounds are robust as they anchor community, inform liturgical practices, and prompt spiritual and numerical growth.

That acts of creative disruption are attributed to the work of the Holy Spirit should be distinguished from what the Lutheran Confessions describe as *Schwärmer*. The Reformers' concern for enthusiasm—those raving verifications of salvation apart from the operative means of the Spirit, God's Word and sacraments—does not negate, however, the fact that God through the Word is dynamically alive in the church (Heb. 4:12). As a corollary, even though the liturgical assembly constitutes a proper arena through which these means are communicated, this does not imply that worship forms themselves cannot be creatively disrupted if they deteriorate into lip service (Matt. 15:9).

A Historical Witness and Martyred Disrupter

Gudina Tumsa, of the Oromo ethnic group, was born in extreme economic poverty in western Ethiopia in 1929, the same year as Martin Luther King Jr. He was martyred on July 28, 1979, at the hands of a brutalizing Marxist revolutionary government. Candid rhetoric, cheerful fearlessness, and courageous witness in the name of Jesus were his traits despite his hardship, suffering, and persecution. Edu-

2. Kolb, "Contemporary Lutheran Understandings," 159.

cated at Luther Seminary in St. Paul, Minnesota, in the 1960s, Tumsa was also a student of the civil rights movement in the United States. He opted for a Martin Luther King Jr.–like strategy of identifying structural sin, mobilizing people of faith, and then working non-violently (which is not passivity) within human institutions, not to overthrow them, but to improve them gradually from within.

Upon his return to his homeland and the Ethiopian Evangelical Church Mekane Yesus (EECMY), Tumsa rose quickly in leadership. This dynamically burgeoning Lutheran church body, headquartered in Addis Ababa, embodies its name "Mekane Yesus," which means in the Amharic language "place of Jesus." Its membership grew from 65,000 members in 1959 to 2.5 million by 1999 (larger than the LCMS), to more than 5 million in 2009 (larger than the Evangelical Lutheran Church of America [ELCA]). Since 2009, the EECMY has grown by more than 1 million people. Lutheranism is vibrant with a bright future on the African continent.[3] In 2016, it had more than 7 million members. Brimming with joy in the power and promises of the gospel, their integration of service and witness, the proximity of the practice of these marks of the church, and their willingness to suffer for their faith have historically characterized their church body and offered an example for the reimagining of Reformation traditions in the global North. Another early African church leader, Tertullian, was right: "the blood of the martyrs is the seed of the Church."[4]

In the 1970s, Tumsa served as the general secretary of the EECMY. Refusing to bow down to the draconian political demands

---

3. There are twice as many Lutherans there as Lutherans on the continent of North America and more Lutherans in two East African nations, Ethiopia and Tanzania, than in Germany. Two summarizing demographic facts that add a facet of perspective on the typical Western view of Lutheranism: (1) There are more Lutherans alive now than ever in the history of the world, and (2) the average global Lutheran now looks like an Ethiopian.

4. Tertullian, *Apologeticus* 50. See Robert D. Sider, *Christian and Pagan in the Roman Empire: The Witness of Tertullian* (Washington, DC: Catholic University of America Press, 2001).

of the revolutionary government seeking to silence the church, he was arrested. Refusing to submit or recant, he was tortured. Refusing to flee from Ethiopia while he had a chance (like Dietrich Bonhoeffer in Nazi Germany), he was rearrested and viciously murdered. Each refusal was predicated on his doctrinal conviction: that God's justice in the world and God's justifying act in Christ are inextricably linked. He wrote:

> The Gospel of Jesus Christ is God's power to save everyone who believes it. It is the power that saves from eternal damnation, from economic exploitation, and from political oppression. . . . It is the only voice telling about a loving Father who gave his Son as a ransom for many. It tells about the forgiveness of sins and the resurrection of the body. It is the Good News to sinful humanity. . . . It is too powerful to be compromised by any social or political system.[5]

Generational Dynamic

There is a generational aspect to tolerance for and expectation of creative disruption that may also be a global phenomenon similar to what motivated Tumsa. I have observed a considerable elasticity in the ecclesiology of those who are digital natives—as contrasted with digital immigrants. Perhaps this is correlated to the developing world's nimble witness, missional creativity, and embrace of the poetics of disruption. Those with fewer physical and concrete investments have smaller portfolios—by portfolios I am referring not only

5. Gudina Tumsa, "The Role of a Christian in a Given Society," in *Revolution and Religion in Ethiopia: The Growth and Persecution of the Mekane Yesus Church, 1974-85*, ed. Oeyvind Eide (Oxford: J. Currey, 2000), 200-204. See also Tumsa's "Memorandum to Ato Emmanuel Abraham, President, ECMY; from Gudina Tumsa, General Secretary, ECMY Re: Some Issues Requiring Discussions and Decisions," 271-79, in the same volume.

to financial assets, but the entire range of the goods to which one is attached, which one carries (*portare*) through life—those goods that become "bad" when used to violate the first commandment.

Once while lecturing on this in a classroom of twenty-some-things, I was struck by the extent to which their awareness of creative disruption was textured by the frequency of technological innovation in their lives—the rapid cycles of interruption by its introduction. Their lives were rarely lived in the realm of complacency except when associating with those unfamiliar with new technology and frequent innovation. This acknowledgment seems to suggest that creative disruption is not a concept posited on the axis of liberal or conservative;[6] rather it is posited demographically—generationally and geographically.

Institutional Wisdom

One of the most difficult aspects in the calling to lead a Christian organization is the negative consequences of being creatively disruptive in a destructive manner. Christians are often conditioned, not wrongly, to be peacemakers and bridge-builders who value highly doing things decently and in good order. The normal human aversion to conflict seems amplified in Christ-followers. That one might actively nurture disruption seems contradictory to middle-class Western notions of what it means to be "nice" Christian leaders. The examples of Tumsa and Bonhoeffer[7]—as martyrs, witnesses

6. If, however, we are speaking of the LCMS, I have long maintained that the range of the axis is from ultra-conservative to moderate. There are very few LCMS-ers who are theologically liberal.

7. "There is no way to peace along the way of safety. For peace must be dared, it is itself the great venture, and can never be safe. Peace is the opposite of security. To demand guarantees is to mistrust, and this mistrusting in turn brings forth war. To look for guarantees is to want to protect oneself. Peace means giving oneself completely to God's commandment, wanting no security, but in faith and obedience

to the way of the cross in sacrificial service—provides biographical material in support of this.

Think of the prayers that liturgical churches pray in Advent, "Stir up your power and come" and "Stir up your might and come." These echo the psalmist who pleads, "Stir up your might and come to save us. Restore us, O God" (Ps. 80:2b–3a). Ponder what is being prayed for here—things being stirred up.

Consider the prayer Jesus taught his followers and their spiritual descendants to pray, especially the petition "your kingdom come." God's realm of holiness cannot enter the unholy realms of this earth without some interruption to business as usual, without some scraping, some reordering, some turning of things upside down. G. K. Chesterton (1874–1936) once described how the coming of Christianity did not, by any means, do away with the traditional patriarchal family, but merely turned it upside down. Instead of moving from father to mother to child, the Holy Family moved from child (Jesus) to Mother Mary to Father God. He then concluded with a quote that has become epigrammatic and applied to many other scenarios: "many things are made holy by being turned upside down."[8] Those words are worth framing as a reminder above one's desk.

Repentance—which typifies the Christian life on a daily basis—is itself sometimes seismic and painful and always includes, humanly speaking, some element of loss, some facing of hard truth: "There can be no redemption unless the truth about the world is told and justice is done. To treat sin as if it were not there, when in fact it is there, amounts to living as if the world were redeemed when in fact it is not."[9] In our devastatingly broken world, Chris-

---

laying down the destiny of the nations in the hand of Almighty God, not trying to direct it for selfish purposes. Battles are won, not with weapons, but with God. They are won when the way leads to the cross." Quoted from Renate Bethge, *Dietrich Bonhoeffer: A Brief Life* (Minneapolis: Augsburg Fortress, 1991), 33–35.

8. G. K. Chesterton, *Heretics* (Rockville, MD: Serenity, 2009), 92.

9. Miroslav Volf, *Exclusion and Embrace: A Theological Exploration of Identity, Otherness, and Reconciliation* (Nashville: Abingdon, 1996), 294.

tian leaders must dare to be creatively disruptive of the patterns, lifestyles, cultural habits, excesses, and oppression that are not God-pleasing. True Christian leaders cannot avoid this prophetic dimension. They are called to call individuals, organizations, staffs, the community, and the world to turn around, for Christ's sake.

This is not advocating being disruptive for its own sake, stirring up dissension for the sake of one's personal agenda or emotional needs or to get even; Proverbs 15:18 warns: "Those who are hot-tempered stir up strife." Rather, we who are in pursuit of excellence, of best practices, of missions that transform hearts, metamorphose minds, and renew relationships with forgiveness, must ourselves be transformed by rekindling "the gift of God that is within you" (2 Tim. 1:6). This verb, "rekindle" in biblical Greek, is composed of three words: *ana* (again), *zōē* (life), *pyreō* (to burn): to burn back to life, restore the fire (Ps. 80:3), relight or reignite the fire, to resurrect, *anastasis*, to light the fire that helps others to see their way forward—that is a responsibility of the leader.

Creative disruption is

- surgical, not random
- scalpel, not sledgehammer
- managed, not unintentional
- careful, not reckless
- prayerful, not self-sufficient
- missional, not self-indulgent
- systemic, not atomistic
- complex, not simplistic
- pruning, not cutting
- generative, not destructive
- oxygenizing, not suffocating
- life-giving, not death-dealing

Tips in Truth Speaking and Creative Disruption from John the Baptizer

What can truth speakers learn from the ministry of this grasshopper-eating, camel hair–wearing, full-throttled, eschaton-preparing, Isaiah-echoing, fire-repentance, wilderness-preaching prophet who comes to stir things up (Luke 3:1–20)?

1. Speaking God's truth is often unpopular, a solitary activity; don't be surprised when you feel like a voice crying in the wilderness.
2. Truth speakers must avoid both the temptation toward self-righteousness and the traumatizing victimhood of self-pity.
3. Truth speakers often convey their message in metaphors—the in-filling of valleys, leveling of mountains, straightening of crooked ways, smoothing over of rough places.
4. Truth speakers stir up the established in-circle with diversity so that all flesh sees the salvation of God.

Rooted in the Death and Resurrection of Jesus

The paramount event of creative disruption is startling and counter-intuitive. Even to consider the sequence of events in Holy Week is to contemplate the most apical, brain-bending, meaning-making moment in world history. While the creative act in Genesis disrupted the primordial chaos of prehistory, this redemptive interruption constitutes an even greater work, according to Bernard: "The work of re-creation and rebuilding is greater than the work of creation and building."[10]

God's intervention for human salvation happens ironically,

10. Bernard, *Loci Theologici*, trans. J. A. O. Preus (St. Louis: Concordia, 1989), 154.

even amid the injustice of Roman colonial violence. There are numerous disruptive implications of Jesus's death, myriad ways it disturbs the status quo. The crucifixion shatters human fixations with worldly fascinations—like obtaining material possessions, maintaining political power, or maximizing physical pleasure. The death of the very icon of God, the One whose coming restores fully the divine image in human identity, disrupts our fabrications that attempt to remake God in our own image. The resurrection of Jesus represents an unpredictable intrusion on complacent religiosity. It resists being printed in the bulletin. It is actuarially ridiculous.

Those who believe it are carried away in an unspeakable sway; they shout "Hallelujah." They are transported by faith, their sanctified imaginations now redefining reality, incorporating people previously sworn off as off limits. Old boundaries fall away. Lepers and the leper-like are healed by God's love. Outsiders gain access. The joyless are leaping in ecstasy. Powerbrokers are broken in repentance. The intimidating territories of the brave and strong no longer terrorize the weak and fearful. Lion and lamb share terrain. Categories no longer exclude. Tax collectors are not only challenged, but by God's incalculable grace also volunteer to change. Privileges are not only upended but also willingly surrendered. Idolatrous priorities are forsaken—the energy once committed to selfishness is now redirected for the good of others. Sinners are welcomed home and transformed by an unanticipated hospitality. Fragmented communities discover new forgiveness-fueled friendships. Dying people are loved to a life that goes beyond their last breath. Human dignity is respected at every age and stage of biology, from every mother's womb to the moment of entrance into Mother Earth's tomb.

All of this incurs disruption, but it is creative disruption because it ennobles us, calling us to our highest selves and fashioning before our very eyes a portrait of eternity.

CHAPTER 5

From Selfies to Selfless

The Way of the Cross as Joyful Diakonia

The social phenomena of Facebook and the ability to take instant pictures of ourselves have created the popularity of selfies in our day. There are people today, especially among our young generation, who have arranged for selfies during their funerals. Many funeral directors today are at odds on how to deal with this practice. Selfies are our fifteen minutes of fame in a world that is turned to itself. I am amazed that even from Cuba, my homeland, I receive requests on Facebook from cousins to friend them and then I find them posting many selfies of themselves on their Facebook page. I realize that not everyone has this ability. Many countries and thousands of people in the United States do not have the means or desire in their hand-to-mouth existence to worry about their virtual lives. But selfies have become a way of life for millions in their everyday existence. They have become in the twentieth-first century a sign of the times of our self-absorption and our self-importance. I would say to this: *mea culpa*. I am also to blame in this state of affairs. However, this turning into self-absorption is not only the malady of individuals. It is also the malady present within our churches and society. Presently, we have millions of refugees from the Middle East seeking asylum, children dying of hunger, and the poor fighting to keep their families together with dignity and honor. This takes place even within the affluence of the United States. US Latino families find themselves also in a crisis due to this state of affairs. This is the sign of the times. The question is: what does the message of the Reformation have to do in our present state of affairs? What does it have to offer?

The Catholic Church and the LWF have already highlighted in the document *From Conflict to Communion* how our commemoration of the Reformation is an opportune time to consider how we can move from self-absorption to service. This is highlighted under the fifth imperative: "Catholics and Lutherans should witness together to the mercy of God in proclamation and service to the world."[1] This document in fact exhorts all Christian churches to engage in this practice. This chapter and reflection is directed to the proclamation of the mercy of God in the concrete practice of service to the world. There is no *diakonia* for the Christian church apart from its possession of the sacred cross as a way of life. This is central to Luther's Reformation vision for the church. It was for Luther one of the seven distinctive marks of the Christian church.[2]

Luther affirms this in *On the Councils and the Churches*: "'Blessed are you when men persecute you on my account' (Matthew 5:11). They must be pious, quiet and obedient, and prepared to serve the government and everybody with life and goods, doing no one any harm."[3] This way of the cross marks for Luther the *martyria* (witness) and *diakonia* (service) of the church for the sake of our society and world at all times and in all places. In reading the Gospels, in particular Mark and Matthew, we find that this is central to the constitutive way of life for the disciples: "For even the Son of Man did not come to be served, but to serve [*diakonēthēnai*], and to give his life as a ransom for many" (Mark 10:45; cf. Matt. 20:28). This way of life is crucial and central in Luther's Reformation theology.

1. *FCTC*, 88.

2. This reflection is found in Luther's well-known treatise *On the Councils and the Churches* (1539) (*LW* 41:164).

3. *LW* 41:164–65.

It is not merely doing things for others. It is a life driven by the love of God to serve others, even to the point of great sacrifice. This is the mark of true discipleship that is accentuated by *diakonia* in the New Testament.[4]

We find this way of service emphasized in Luther's Heidelberg Theses (1518) and his *Operationes in Psalmos* (1519–21). These works have been subject to numerous studies.[5] The way of the cross does not engage in a mere explanation of what salvation is all about. It rather emphatically shatters our pride and the building of our towers of Babel. Christ's cross wakes us from our slumber of self-importance to serve God in the world. The way of the cross is not a mere empty exercise in suffering, for it is grounded in the concrete exercise of God's love. This way of the cross needs to be exercised in our service with others, and not merely in our ministry for others in the church and world. This is an important nuance and difference in how we engage in *diakonia*. This *diakonia* under the cross reimagines and accentuates the way of service in a different way. It is a way of service that does not begin at the center in theory and practice. *Diakonia* does not begin with how we think we will benefit others. It does not start from the tall order of our self-importance. It is an incarnational walking and standing with others in their distress, anguish, and need. It is a living *diakonia* in everyday life (*en lo cotidiano*) with others. This is how a *diakonia* from the margins and the borderlands lives the faith.

This way of service has been accentuated by Latin American

4. See "*Diakonēo* in the N.T.," in *Theological Dictionary of the New Testament,* ed. Gerhard Kittel (Grand Rapids: Eerdmans, 1964), 2:84–85.

5. There are a number of studies that point to this. For current proposals on this topic, see Vitor Westhelle, *The Scandalous God: The Use and Abuse of the Cross* (Minneapolis: Fortress, 2009); Hinlicky, *Luther and the Beloved Community*, 301–78; Mary M. Solberg, *Compelling: A Feminist Proposal for an Epistemology of the Cross* (New York: State University of New York Press, 1997), 55–94; Alberto L. García, "Signposts for Global Witness in Luther's Theology of the Cross," in *The Theology of the Cross for the 21st Century*, ed. Alberto L. García and A. R. Victor Raj (St. Louis: Concordia, 2002), 15–36.

theologians since the late 1960s. Leonardo Boff emphasizes how the *diakonia* of the people of God must be carried out: "Thus, it no longer entails the Church for the poor but rather a Church of the poor and with the poor."[6] Boff underscores in the same breath and formula that *koinōnia* (shared community and communion) belongs together with *diakonia* and "prophecy" (i.e., prophetic witness) in this biblical service to the poor.[7] In other words, there is no *diakonia*, service, toward the poor and the broken, unless we walk with them and participate with them with a prophetic voice against their marginal existence. Boff approximates in a way what US Latino and Latina theologians have been affirming for the past thirty years. Our witness and service begin from our *convivir*, our life together, in the margins. Surprisingly enough, signs for this way of service may be perceived in Luther's 95 Theses, posted on October 31, 1517, on the Castle Church door in Wittenberg. They need to be reimagined, however, in light of our present pilgrimage in the world. First, however, we must listen to Luther's insights.

The 95 Theses Call for *Diakonia* at the Margins

There are many romantic or popular explanations for why Luther planted his 95 Theses on the doors of the *Schlosskirche* in Wittenberg. We have read biographies where Luther is found searching for a merciful God and for peace in the Scriptures due to his personal

6. Leonardo Boff, *Iglesia: carisma y poder* (Santander: Sal Terrae, 1981), 25–26. Boff's perspective, however, is a practice carried out within the economic, social, and political life of the people. It does not address the problem of identity that is a critical issue for our marginal living experience in the Americas. For a perceptive understanding of this difference, see Michelle A. González, "Is Pope Francis the First Latin American Pope? The Politics of Identity in America," in *Pope Francis in Postcolonial Reality*, ed. Nicolas Panotto (Borderless, 2015), 77–86. González's critique takes into consideration the issue of identity as discussed in the first chapter of this book.

7. Boff, *Iglesia*, 25.

angst. There is a truth to this. There is also the belief that once Luther "discovered the gospel" he put his fighting gloves on against the false teachings of the church. Many popular accounts underscore this to be the main reason Luther wrote and posted his 95 Theses at Wittenberg. This is not really the story behind these theses.

When Luther wrote his 95 Theses he already had a clear vision that the gospel offered first and foremost the gift of God's grace and mercy in the person of Jesus Christ to a sinful world. He writes in Thesis 62: "The true treasure of the church is the most holy gospel of the glory and grace of Christ."[8] This was not, however, the end of the story for Luther on this matter. Throughout his life and writings, we find him struggling with his own humanness and sin. We find a blessed paradox where Luther knew that God is for us and not against us. At the same time, however, he knew that sin permeates our whole life. We are totally sinful and totally justified. God calls us to daily repentance through our baptism. In this remembrance and prayer, we die to sin daily and arise to serve others daily by the power of the Holy Spirit. Luther lived in this paradox and struggle all his life. Luther made sure that he taught this to the faithful in his *Small Catechism* (1529).[9] This daily action of repentance is necessary in renewing our daily vocations to care within our families, our communities, and the world around us. Luther's intent in the posting of the 95 Theses was grounded in his pastoral concern for the people of God in light of these acquired insights. The gospel offers a God for us. Not only was this precious gift of the gospel being set aside, but the church's actions were also oppressing the faithful, especially those at the margins, through the selling of indulgences. How was this happening?

8. See *LW* 31:230. Luther makes this perfectly clear in his *Explanations of the Ninety-Five Theses* published in 1518 (see *LW* 31:230–31). This is also poignantly expressed in Luther's *Disputation against Scholastic Theology*, written in September 1518, a month before the 95 Theses. See in particular his Theses 40 and 43 (*LW* 31:12–13).

9. *BC*, 360–61.

The church's illusory claim at the time was that it was serving the people best through its offer of indulgences. The faithful bought this claim hook, line, and sinker. They also believed that they were serving their church and their Christian life best by buying these indulgences. The faithful began to believe that this was the way to find security and peace for eternal life. Luther's intention in posting the theses was neither to begin a reformation movement nor to break away from the church. He did not actually attack in this document the pastoral system established by the Catholic Church in order to mercifully mitigate the penances for sin imposed by the church.[10] Luther knew, however, how the selling of indulgences destroyed the very essence of the gospel as a gift from God and also paralyzed the service that Christians must live out under the cross. This is why he wrote with a pastoral heart against the improper use of indulgences. This had become an important and decisive time for Luther because the selling of indulgences had been intensified in his homeland.[11] He could no longer keep silent. Luther had a passion for service in the way of the cross.

10. This is neither the time nor the place to discuss the Catholic Church's sacrament of penance, or the system of indulgences in the sixteenth century, a system that Luther later abandoned. For an easy and readable explanation of the Catholic teaching on the sacrament of penance, and Luther's dialogue with the use and practice of the sacrament at the time, as well as an overview of other theologians in the fifteenth and sixteenth centuries, see James Atkinson, *Martin Luther and the Birth of Protestantism* (Atlanta: John Knox, 1968), 142–56. We must caution the reader that indulgences do not mean the same thing to Catholics today as they did to Luther and his contemporaries and Catholicism five hundred years ago.

11. Pope Leo X (1475–1521) was strapped for funds at the time due to his ambitious desire to rebuild Saint Peter's Basilica in the grandiose style that princes and kings during the Renaissance expected and demanded. His opportune time came when Albrecht von Brandenburg (1490–1545) had to find a way to pay for his debt acquired from Jacob Fugger for the fees already paid to Rome for his holy seat. He was also bound with more contributions to the Basilica project. This created chaos for the faithful and also for the merchants in Germany. See Kittelson, *Luther*, 101–8; Eric W. Gritsch, *Reformer without a Church: The Life and Thought of Thomas Muentzer (1488?–1525)* (Philadelphia: Fortress, 1967).

Luther writes in Thesis 50: "Christians are to be taught that if the pope knew the exactions of the indulgence preachers, he would rather that the Basilica of St. Peter were burned to ashes than built up with the skin, flesh, and bones of his sheep."[12] There is a definite call for *diakonia* with the people in the margins in this thesis. The pope, who was Luther's primary spiritual leader and pastor at the time, was being called to engage as shepherd of his people at the very margins. He needed to walk with them in their poverty and distress. The very incarnate *diakonia* of the gospel was at stake. The church was being called to move away from its self-service and self-interest. The selling of indulgences was preventing the pastor of the church (as well as other pastors ministering under his leadership), and the very people of God, from walking along with the most vulnerable. In fact, the practice of selling indulgences was hurting the people at the borderlands by promoting the embellishment of the institution. The way of the cross was totally removed from this call of self-service to and for the church. Theses 63 and 64 capture the very essence of Christ's *diakonia* from the margins. We have discovered in Thesis 62 how the holy gospel is the true treasure and the grace of God. Now Theses 63 and 64 crystallize how the *diakonia* of the gospel is played out in light of Matthew 20:16.

Diakonia begins and ends from the very margins of the church and not at the center. For "this treasure . . . makes the first to be last," but indulgences (considering our very needs and desires first) make the one who should be last first.[13] The gospel reverses the order of service in the right order. This is Luther's explanation in Thesis 63: "The gospel destroys those things which exist, it confounds the strong, it confounds the wise and reduces them to nothingness, to weakness, to foolishness, because it teaches humility and a cross."[14] The service of the church begins in living the very weakness of the

12. *LW* 31:30.
13. *LW* 31:31.
14. *LW* 31:32.

cross. It means standing with and not merely for the least of the brethren. This standing with requires risks and even suffering. It is a committed service rather than a service from above. This is the *diakonia* envisioned by Luther in his 95 Theses. This perspective is repeated time and time again in these theses. It is forcefully hammered in through Theses 43–46. The poor and the struggling families are more important than what benefits the church for its own advancement.[15] We must live with them in the margins rather than "serve" them for our own sake.

Luther, therefore, is looking outward, but also incarnationally, on how to walk in service in the world. Luther concludes his 95 Theses by focusing on how the servant church lives under the cross:

92. Away then with all those prophets who say to the people of Christ, "Peace, peace," and there is no peace! [Jer. 6:14].
93. Blessed be all those prophets who say to the people of Christ, "Cross, cross," and there is no cross!
94. Christians should be exhorted to be diligent in following Christ, their head, through penalties, death, and hell;
95. And thus be confident of entering into heaven through many tribulations rather than through the false security of peace [Acts 14:22].[16]

Luther does not offer an explanation of these last four theses in his *Explanations of the 95 Theses* that he published in 1518. I believe that the reason is obvious. Luther finds that these four concluding theses are clear as to their meaning and message. It is obvious that Luther in this context wants to unmask the idolatrous false sense of certainty concerning our salvation. He also wants to unmask the church's false pretense concerning its service to the people. The church at the time believed that it was serving the faithful best

15. *LW* 31:29.
16. *LW* 31:33.

with the selling of indulgences. For those who taught that we have certainty of God's mercy for us through this selling and buying of indulgences, Luther's response is "Away then with all those prophets who say to the people of Christ, 'Peace, peace,' and there is no peace" (Thesis 92). There is no salvation, no true service to Christ and the world, when we focus on what peace we can buy for ourselves.

Luther then offers the paradox of the theologian of the cross in the following thesis. "Blessed be all those prophets who say to the people of Christ, 'Cross, cross,' and there is no cross." This is the fact of the matter for the theologian of the cross. When we engage incarnationally in service to others, and their tribulations, this way of the cross may spell out sufferings and tribulations. This is, however, the way of peace because we live in the life of the crucified and risen Christ. Theses 94 and 95 confirm and clarify this vision further. Boff's already shared insights apply here. This way of the cross engages in a radical prophetic proclamation of the cross that may spell out martyrdom. This *diakonia*, this way of the cross, is what brings us true peace.

Luther's theology of the cross seems to be quite morbid to many contemporaries. In fact, even some of the best contemporary apologetics attempts seem to spend an inordinate amount of time on the death and suffering dimensions of Christ's cross. They also seem to dwell on Luther's claim that God struggled against God on the cross. This is particularly accentuated in Vitor Westelle's *The Scandalous God* as he concludes chapter 3 of his book:[17] "Here we have an invitation to face with hope, but a hope against all hope, the terrible void, the *horror vacui* of a God that, according to our perception, cannot be but the One who is against God. In Luther's words: *ad deum contra deum confungere*, 'to flee from and find refuge in God against God.'"[18] My purpose here is not to contradict Westhelle or

---

17. Westhelle, *The Scandalous God*, 35–59. This is chapter 3, "God against God: Reformation, Then and Now" (cf. WA 5:204.26f.).

18. Westhelle, *The Scandalous God*, 59.

to engage in pursing another apologetics for Luther's theology of the cross. I agree that it is a theology of paradox and suffering. However, there is a strong tradition, going back to Augustine, where there is a powerful bond and union between the Father and the Son through their relationship with the Holy Spirit even at the darkest moment of separation.[19] This is a relationship grounded in God's love and resolve to serve the world. The Holy Spirit is present as a gift of God's presence in this relationship. The Spirit is also present as gift in the mission of the church. This is how for Luther the *diakonia* of the cross lives out in the world. It lives in God's joy through the presence of the Holy Spirit and the hope of the resurrection (Acts 2:33) in spite of our human anguish.

God is very much present in our *compañerismo* (walking together) in mutual service in the world. Luther offers hints of this in his comments on Galatians 4:6.[20] God is present in our walking with those in the margins in the name of the crucified and risen Christ by the unequivocal presence of the Spirit. It is in light of

19. Cf. Luis F. Ladaria, *The Living and True God: The Mystery of the Trinity* (Miami: Convivium, 2010), 111–16. These are Ladaria's observations: "If the abandonment of Jesus by the Father can express the 'distance,' the differentiation of the person in God, which is at its maximum, the obedience of the Son, the acceptance of the Father's plan and radical trust in him show the deep unity and divine communion. The two aspects must be seen in unity. Any separation, as great as we can and should think it, cannot make us forget that the Father and Son are in pure reference to one another" (115). Ladaria points out how this dynamic is present among many contemporary theologians. However, Jurgën Moltmann, contrary to other theologians, such as Eberhard Jüngel, tends to maintain this *horror vacui*. Luther does not dwell on an ongoing vacuity but affirms it as God's position for us as he moves on in affirming the work of the Holy Spirit.

20. Luther writes in *Lectures on Galatians* (1535) (*LW* 26:380): "The Spirit of Christ sent by God into our hearts, cries: 'Abba! Father!' . . . He helps us in our weakness and intercedes for us. . . . Anyone who truly believed this would not fall into affliction, no matter how great. So when we cry feeling God's absence because of our present tribulation, God's Spirit presents itself with a word of hope and consolations." See also Luther's comments in his Galatians commentary (1519) (*LW* 27:290–91).

God's joyful consolation and peace rather than his absence in despair that God serves in the midst of the world. This point of departure is present in Luther's vocation of the cross. This is an important point of departure for the reimagining of our *diakonia* within US Latino communities.

I want to accent Luther's primary foundation for our vocation of the cross in light of our Christian baptism. In his *Large Catechism* (1529), Luther unequivocally affirms that the "power, fruit, and benefit of baptism is that it saves us." But "to be saved" includes both "being delivered from sin" and the benefit of "enter[ing] God's kingdom."[21] We are received in this act in the name of the Triune God and by the action of the Holy Spirit "into the Christian community."[22] Luther lays out how the vocation of the cross plays out in a sermon he preached in Augsburg ca. 1518–19.[23] Gustaf Wingren in his classic book *Luther on Vocation* underscores the importance of our *diakonia* under the cross by way of reflection on this sermon. This sermon is referred to in the English translation of this work as a "treatise."[24] This is incorrect. Luther wrote his treatises mostly for theologians and rulers. Sermons were proclaimed front and center before the congregations. Therefore, we find that Luther envisions these themes as essential foundations for the life of the priesthood of all believers. This is also why I made special reference above to Luther's *Small* and *Large Catechisms*. The *diakonia* of the faithful in the world is the very essence of being Christians and being the church.

How is our vocation of the cross acted out in light of Luther's "Sermon on the Holy Most Precious Sacrament of Baptism" (1518–

21. *BC*, 459.

22. *BC*, 256. In Latin it reads "in christianorum communionem" (into the *koinōnia*, communion of Christians). *Die Bekenntnis Schriften* (Göttingen: Vandenhoeck & Ruprecht, 1979), 691.

23. "Ein Sermon von dem heiligen hoch wirdigen Sacrament der Taufe" (*WA* 2:727–37).

24. Gustaf Wingren, *Luther on Vocation*, trans. Carl M. Rasmussen (Philadelphia: Muhlenberg, 1957), 28.

19)? Baptism is the "church's fundamental sacrament."[25] Why? Luther reads it in light of Romans 6. The Christian lives daily in the dying to his or her sin and selfishness to rise as a new person for service. This is a daily struggle because of our human condition. Our aim is to live in the hope of God's new creation. We know that our present actions are tentative but we are always focused on the Spirit in the hope of the consummation of God's new creation.[26] Christians live this vocation of the cross in all of our roles as human beings (husbands, wives, citizens, et al.). All Christians have a calling, a vocation, not only pastors, to stand alongside one's neighbor, bearing one's own cross for the sake of others.[27] We also walk along with them and bear their crosses with them. It is, in other words, not a *diakonia* for others but rather a *diakonia* with others. This is central to Luther's understanding of Christ: for Christ is "a Savior who is also our Brother, who is our flesh and blood, who became like us in all respects but sin."[28] God stands with us in solidarity as a family member and not at a distance.

Luther's treatise *Two Kinds of Righteousness* (1519) develops further this way of life and service. I would like to pinpoint how intensely Luther viewed this *diakonia* under the cross in this treatise:

> Paul's meaning is that when each person has forgotten himself and emptied himself of God's gifts, he should conduct himself as if his neighbor's weakness, sin, and foolishness were his very own. He should not boast or get puffed up. Nor should he despise or triumph over his neighbor as if he were his god or equal to God. Since God's prerogatives ought to be left to God

25. Wingren, *Luther on Vocation*, 28 (cf. WA 2:727–28).

26. Tertullian, as well as other church fathers, affirms this as the sine qua non of the supreme act of service in walking with others in witness to the faith, that is, martyrdom. See his explanation of Ephesians 4:20 in his exhortation *Ad Martyres*, in *The Ante-Nicene Fathers* (Buffalo, NY: Christian Literature Company, 1895), 3:693.

27. Wingren, *Luther on Vocation*, 29 (cf. WA 2:729).

28. The quote is from a sermon on John by Luther in 1537 (*LW* 22:24).

alone, it becomes robbery when a man in haughty foolhardiness ignores this fact. It is in this way, then, that one takes the form of a servant, and that command of the Apostle in Gal. 5[:13] is fulfilled: "Through love be servants of one another." Through the figure of the members of the body Paul teaches in Rom. 12[:4–5] and I Cor. 12[:12–27] how the strong, honorable, healthy members do not glory over those that are weak, less honorable, and sick as if they were their masters and gods; but on the contrary they serve them the more, forgetting their own honor, health, and power. For thus no member of the body serves itself; nor does it seek its own welfare but that of the other. And the weaker, the sicker, the less honorable a member is, the more the other members serve it "that there may be no discord in the body, but that the members may have the same care for one another," to use Paul's words [I Cor. 12:25]. From this it is now evident how one must conduct himself with his neighbor in each situation.[29]

The *diakonia* of the Christian and the church—for the church is in Luther's definition "holy believers and 'the little sheep who hear the voice of their shepherd'"[30]—is to live in an incarnate manner the way of the cross with others. It is a *diakonia* within both the body of Christ and the world. In light of the presence of the crucified and risen Christ with us, and in light of the presence of the Holy Spirit with us, we do not live a faith in the high heavens. We live this faith in our walking in the margins with the "weak" and those considered "less honorable." But it is a walking in the joy of the presence of God with us, in spite of our humanness and ambiguities. This is especially brought out in Luther's *Operationes in Psalmos* and his treatise concerning the freedom of a Christian. There may be suffering but

29. *LW* 31:302–3.
30. *BC*, 324. Quoted from the *Smalcald Articles* (1537). Luther is making reference to John 10:3.

we bear the joy of Christ and the presence of the Holy Spirit in our *diakonia* within what Luther calls an *admirable commercium*, or *frohliche Wechsel*, in these works.[31] This is a most "joyous exchange." The wonder of God's presence in our *diakonia* of the cross brings forth this celebration of our common life in walking together in the margins. This is why Luther calls this act a *dulcissimum spectaculum*, the "sweetest of public events." The God of life and not of death walks with us as we render service within our world.

Diakonia in the US Latino Community

How is it in a metaphorical sense that the church is selling and the faithful buying indulgences today? In terms of US Latino ministries I could point to many and various ways that this is present in our context. First and foremost, the most practiced modus operandi for outreach to Hispanics in North America (and for that matter in Latin America) sounds like a selling or buying of indulgences. Why? Mainline denominations and local congregations often engage in outreach out of pure necessity. In the context of all Lutheran denominations in North America the traditional non-Latino membership is declining at a rapid rate. This is also the case for Methodists, Presbyterians, Baptists of different persuasions, and other Christian groups. The main resolve to be involved in outreach to Latinos is to preserve their old grandeur or to maintain it. The investment in ministries among the people in the margins is usually envisioned as a way of "selling indulgences." The number one reason that the US Latino population is being addressed is to build our own churches or membership. There is the tendency to serve others for our own sake rather than to walk with them in their need.

31. See *Operationes in Psalmos* (*WA* 5:608.7) and *The Freedom of a Christian* (*WA* 7:25 and 34).

Many leaders and parishioners within congregations view their church as theirs because they bought it with their offerings. Outreach is envisioned to find ways that outsiders can contribute to preserve their status quo. This is also the outlook of many church judicatories. Many judicatories circle around like piranhas when a particular congregation is going to close their doors. This means that they can sell these buildings and use the money to maintain their status quo. It has been noted, however, that some judicatories, and congregations ready to close their doors, have determined to walk with the people in their communities. They are willing to live by faith under the cross. They have given their buildings over to Latino ministries and those ministries have grown and progressed quite rapidly in a great number of cases.[32]

The same applies to planning and conducting ministry at the margins. Many churches find it necessary to call Latino and Latina pastors to their congregations to minister among their people. However, they also intend that once the first generation, or the Spanish-speaking generation, has passed on, Anglo- or European-descent pastors should take over in ministering to the second and third generations of Latinos. This is another way of selling indulgences. Ministry, *diakonia*, is envisioned as one for the sake of us rather than walking with others in the margins.

There is also the intent to spend some time with those poor people in doing things for them. Give them some clothes and food. Serve once or twice a year in a soup kitchen. Many short-term trips to Central and Latin America are organized for short-term tourism or to do for those poor people what they cannot do for themselves. This is another way of buying indulgences. However, when it comes

---

32. These insights are based on a number of essays in *Our Ninety-Five Thesis: Five Hundred Years after the Reformation*, ed. Justo L. González and Alberto L. García (Asociación para La Educatión Teológica Hispana, 2016). I am drawing from the insights of Isaías A. Rodríguez in his essay "A Reflection Concerning Anglicanism and the Hispanic World"; and Orlando E. Espín, "500 Years after the Posting of Luther's Theses: A Catholic Perspective."

to walking with them hand in hand for the long haul, to stand up incarnationally for their causes, we do not want to pay the cost of carrying our own crosses by walking with them in life and death.

There are many and various ways in which our denominations want to sell indulgences or we as God's people want to buy indulgences only to serve ourselves. US Hispanic congregations are not immune from this malady. I have found, for example, among many independent Latino community congregations, some Pentecostal in character, how they quickly split into many factions. This is because the leaders want the people to buy hook, line, and sinker their own brand and offer of Christianity. This is another form of selling indulgences. The question is: are we willing to walk with our brothers and sisters who cry foul play and are treated as lepers or deranged people in our society because of their marginal existence? Are we willing to extend ourselves under the guidance of the Holy Spirit to walk in concrete service with our communities?

I have known many martyrs of the faith (not necessarily who died in proclaiming the gospel) who have labored intensely and walked along with the people of God at the margins. I could pinpoint people of various nationalities, including many of my Anglo brothers and sisters, who have done so. They do not hide from this life of bearing the cross, of being tested, as they serve in the world. They have found joy in serving under the cross. Their afflictions, *Anfechtungen*, therefore, have to be understood not as the sufferings brought on because of their sins and human condition. These are always there because of our human frailties. This is also a dimension of Luther's understanding of being tested under the cross. The sufferings of the servants of God, however, are also the banner of living incarnationally, of walking along with those at the margins. It is a sign, a banner, that we carry in the name of Jesus of Galilee who walks with us and is for us.[33] It is the kind of walk where we suffer for standing with others in their marginality.

33. Prenter, *Spiritus Creator*, 27–32. See also Luther's comments concerning

Luther affirms that the Holy Spirit comforts and communicates to us that our warfare with God has ended in this strife. Our crosses in our acts of service proclaim the Easter event and the walking of God with us by the presence of the Spirit. Our sufferings should not be regarded as a sign of God's absence. Luther affirms this in his commentary on Psalm 8 in his *Operationes in Psalmos*: "Christ became for us a human being everywhere and in every respect without hope and afflicted. Now he has the Lordship over all things and his rule will be praised, commended and worshipped."[34] How do we live, then, Christ's Lordship within the margins? We turn to the Gospel of John and the book of Acts for some important narratives. These are relevant to our ministry with and not merely for Latinos in the United States. Luther's *diakonia* of the cross may be further understood in light of these images and situations.

The Presence of the Holy Spirit in Our *Diakonia*

Vitor Westhelle offers a constructive proposal to mitigate the absence of God using the insights of the mystical Mexican nun Sor Juana de la Cruz (1651–95).[35] Sor Juana highlights the messianic presence of God in our practice of the faith and not through speculative discourses. There are some positive connections here between Luther and Sor Juana. However, there are some important differences that are crucial for our *diakonia*. Sor Juana offers as a way of

---

Romans 8:3 (*LW* 25:349). Cf. Alberto L. García, "Theology of the Cross: A Critical Study of Leonardo Boff's and Jon Sobrino's Theology of the Cross in Light of Luther's Theology of the Cross as Interpreted by Luther Scholars" (PhD diss., Lutheran School of Theology at Chicago, 1987), 285–305. We often neglect the fact that for Luther the way of the cross is not a mere theology of absence or being afflicted because of our sin. It is a vocation through which we bring forth the joy of the risen Christ in the consolation and power of the Spirit. My dissertation written years ago underscores this point quite clearly.

34. As quoted in Lienhard, *Luther*, 119. The quote is taken from *WA* 5:277.11ff.
35. Westhelle, *The Scandalous God*, 138–39.

explanation the words of Jesus in John 16:7: "Nevertheless I tell you the truth: it is to your advantage that I go away, for if I do not go away, the Advocate [*paraklētos*] will not come to you; but if I go, I will send him to you." Westhelle argues that this presence of God is, in Sor Juana's vision, a paradoxical presence, for God becomes present in his very absence. This is how God is present in us rather than among us. I believe that Luther points to both. But most important, he affirms the joyful presence of the work of the Holy Spirit among us. This is a crucial insight gathered from our Western Trinitarian tradition (Augustine). God, in the person of the Holy Spirit, is always present as a gift to the church.[36] There is a presence of God's purpose, community, love, and joy in the outpouring of the Spirit. God is with us in this manner. We serve and give witness to God in light of this presence.

Luther follows this line of thinking in his sermons on John 16. He comments that there is a joy in the presence of the Holy Spirit in spite of the physical absence of Christ.[37] Luther's comments are offered in light of what it means to live in the service of the gospel. He highlights in his comments on John 16:3 that one of the end results of this service will be that we may be excluded from the center of our communities of faith.[38] The presence of God is one, therefore, where God binds us with him in community, and walks with us because of the presence of the Holy Spirit. It is God walking alongside us through the presence and guidance of the Spirit.[39] We are therefore able not only to care for others but also to speak to others God's prophetic words to unmask and call for change to the present ills endured at the margins. While Lutherans and Pentecostals do not share a unified vision of how the Spirit is present among us, it is important to highlight how this plays out in the Latino communities in the United States.

36. See Ladaria, *The Living and True God*, 360–76. See also note 19.
37. *LW* 24:334–35.
38. *LW* 24:302–16.
39. *LW* 24:334–39.

Pentecostalism has made a great impact on Latinos in the Americas. Pentecostalism has also made great inroads among the US Latino populations. We need to dialogue with this movement seriously in our commemoration of the Reformation. A key element in Pentecostal Christology is the relationship of Jesus Christ to the Holy Spirit. Key to the life and practice of a significant number of Pentecostal communities is how Jesus Christ is our *Divino Compañero*, our "divine companion who walks with us." This is always carried out in his care through the presence of the Holy Spirit. The Son sends forth the Spirit to accompany us in our distress to care for us. Sammy Alfaro's *Divino Compañero: Toward a Hispanic Pentecostal Christology* cites several hymns and *coritos* (popular evangelical songs) where the caring presence of the Holy Spirit lives in the community because of Jesus Christ.[40] There is the joyful presence of the Spirit in spite of people's suffering. This is an integral element of the worship life of many Pentecostal congregations. The book of Acts offers concrete examples of how this way of service with others is essential for the Christian church.

Acts 2:43–47 describes how after Pentecost the early church gathered not only in prayer but also in service by walking and living together: "All who believed were together and had all things in common; they would sell their possessions and goods and distribute the proceeds to all, as any had need. Day by day, as they spent much time together in the temple, they broke bread at home and ate their food with glad and generous hearts, praising God and having the goodwill of all the people." Fellowship was carried out with a conscious effort toward mutual service for one another. The joy of the Holy Spirit was present in this manner in spite of the many challenges they faced.

40. Sammy Alfaro, *Divino Compañero: Toward a Hispanic Pentecostal Christology*, Princeton Theological Monograph Series (Eugene, OR: Wipf and Stock, 2010). See chapter 4, "*Divino Compañero*: Toward a Hispanic Pentecostal Christology." See also Luis E. Benavides, "The Spirit," in *Handbook of Latina/o Theologies*, ed. Edwin David Aponte and Miguel A. De La Torre (St. Louis: Chalice, 2006), 29–31.

Acts 6:1–7 reveals how this way of life was challenged and how it was overcome. The event of Pentecost opened the door for the Hellenists (Jewish people from the diaspora) to hear the gospel and become members of the Christian church (Acts 2:5–12, 38–41). These Hellenists were raised away from Palestine in the eastern Mediterranean region and, therefore, found themselves more at ease with Greek. Aramaic was the main language spoken by the Hebrews in Palestine. The apostles, who are referred as "Galileans" in Acts 2:7, in essence spoke the dominant language for Christianity at the time, which was Aramaic. These facts are important to note. In spite of the fact that Jesus was a Galilean and his apostles were from Galilee, these apostles, in spite of their marginality in their society and religious world, had become the center of power for the early Christian church. The church at Jerusalem, its apostles, and Aramaic, their spoken language, had become the dominant factors in the ministry of the church. It was a ministry of insiders to outsiders. This was a *diakonia from* rather than *with* the new marginal members of the Christian community. All generations require this realization, that those who once were at the margins may become one day the brokers of power and service. It is imperative, therefore, that all generations engage in the reimagining of *diakonia* from the margins.

The ministry of insiders to outsiders requires a radical reimagining. This is clearly noted in Acts 6:1–2: "Now during those days, when the disciples were increasing in number, the Hellenists complained against the Hebrews because their widows were being neglected in the daily distribution of food." The text is clear that there was a *diakonia*, a service being made for the marginal Hellenist Christian community. It was being carried out by the dominant church, from their perspective of service and mainly in light of their customs and language. But now because of the pluralism of cultures thanks to the gift of the Holy Spirit, "the Hellenists complained against the Hebrews." This complaint necessitated the reimagining of service in light of the work of the Holy Spirit. Those who follow a paradigm from the center would mainly point out that the apostles merely turned over some of their many duties to seven "deacons" (they were really not called "deacons" although the apostles laid hands and consecrated them for ministry [6:6]). They did this in order that they "should not neglect the word of God" (6:2). But there is a greater vision for service here.

First, the apostles were willing to turn over an important aspect of their ministry to faithful disciples under the guidance of the Holy Spirit. They also followed the lead of the Holy Spirit by turning this ministry over to seven Hellenists. Note that the seven have Greek names. One of them, Nicolas from Antioch, was a convert to Judaism (6:5). In other words, one of them was a Greek-speaking Gentile who had converted to Judaism. There was a great shift and move out of the sandbox under the guidance of the Holy Spirit. The Holy Spirit guided the Galilean apostles to listen to the cries from the margins. There was injustice in the distribution of the goods and the apostles listened to the Hellenists. They entrusted the authority and the direction of this ministry of service to those at the margins. It became a ministry no longer from the apostles to the needy. It became a ministry of walking alongside those who suffered by empowering them to conduct this ministry in light of their struggles, concerns, and needs. It was no longer a service done for the sake of those doing ministry from the center. It was a *diakonia* in light of the cries from the margins. The people from the margins had an investment and a say in the work of God. This is the critical point of departure for our reimagining of *diakonia* from the margins. The early church was able to go beyond its own borders of service because its members ministered by walking with the people at the margins as the Holy Spirit guided them. It was not a *diakonia* of selling indulgences but rather a *diakonia* of openness, risk, and vulnerability by walking with others.[41] This was a critical

41. See Justo L. González, *Acts*, 88–94, for more specific annotations on Acts 6. Some other commentaries offer similar hints but do not fully develop this

component that facilitated the spread of the gospel in the early church (Acts 7–8).

Justo González in his commentary on Acts reflects how the same issues faced in Acts 6 by the church are faced today in Latin America and US Hispanic ministries. I already pointed out above from my own experiences how this has played out in my context. The dominant church must learn to reimagine its way of service in light of Luther's vision and the book of Acts. We need to listen and empower the margins for ministry. Otherwise we continue in many and various ways the deplorable practice of selling indulgences in the twenty-first century. This requires reimagining our *diakonia* in light of the vocation of the cross. This is not a solemn dutiful action but rather a new resolve to follow the way of the cross as a joyful *diakonia* within the margins. I pray that the cries from our US Latino communities from the margins be heard in our resolve to engage in our service with them at this *kairos*. This should be our resolve in seeking the renewal of the Reformation gospel for our time and day.

---

shift from a "*diakonia* for" to a "*diakonia* with" the new converts. See, for example, John B. Polhill, *The New American Commentary: Acts* (Nashville: Broadman and Holman, 1992), 26:177.

CHAPTER 6

Diakonia

....

Witness, Service, and Life Together

The 1995 Mission Affirmations of the LCMS open with a prayer that was read at the beginning of the report of the Floor Committee on Missions:

> Help us to see ourselves as your mission to people in their every need, to society in all its tensions, to the church in all its tribulation and to the whole world in all its futile struggles to find its peace without you. Give us, who are your sent ones, your compassion for your lost ones.[1]

This prayer shines conspicuously in its affirmation of various ministries supporting evangelistic witness in a constellation of interrelated action. It is a petition speaking directly to the unique, salvific wholeness found only in Jesus Christ. It exudes a wide-eyed sensitivity to the various contexts of mission. It avows its intent to be in solidarity with human struggle against sin and suffering.

1. The language has been updated. This is how the text originally read in the Mission Affirmations (1965): "Help us to see ourselves as Thy mission to men in their every need, to society in all its tensions, to the church in all its tribulation and to the whole world in all its futile struggles to find its peace without Thee. Give us, who are Thy sent ones, Thy compassion for Thy lost ones."

Overall, these words reflect the life and ministry of Jesus in whom there was no distinction between fervor for the lost and compassion for the "least of these." Multiple times we hear variations on how he accomplished his mission: "Jesus went throughout Galilee, teaching in their synagogues and proclaiming the good news of the kingdom and curing every disease and every sickness among the people" (Matt. 4:23).

While many positive changes since 1965 have strengthened the practices of the LCMS's faith-based development work and mission activities, the escalation of a professionalized approach raises a potential concern. Techniques imported uncritically from disciplines external to the church have, in part, led to a disconnection of the various componential functions. This, coupled with the tendency of Westerners to prefer tidy siloes in life, that is, sacred and secular—which perhaps is intensified among Lutherans who hold to a binary interpretation of the doctrine of two kingdoms—has not resulted in the best outcome with respect to mission.

Standards have risen, arguably, and foci become clearer, but the result has also been an either/or dilemma: either human care ministries (*diakonia*) or evangelism (*martyria*). Further, the proximity between proclamation (*kērygma*) and expressions of ecclesia (*koinōnia*) with diaconal activity has lessened. This chapter proposes a theological approach for the de-departmentalization of these marks of the church recoupled with a recovery of what the epigraphic prayer asks God for—the gift of eyes to see the church's mission comprehensively especially as Western Lutherans learn from their sisters and brothers in the developing world.

The term *missio trinitatis*[2] is proposed as a framework in nu-

---

2. I initially became familiar with the notion of *missio trinitatis* in conversation with Mike Breen in Palm Springs, California, in September 2015 during our shared ride to the airport. Breen uses this term to describe families in missional activity, in contrast to *missio dei*, which he considers individualistic. See Michael Breen and Sally Breen, *Family on Mission* (Pawleys Island: 3DM, 2014). This term is also employed and explicated in the work of Peter Bellini, assistant professor in

anced contrast with the *missio Dei*. The image of God, inherent in all humans, cannot be either understood or realized by Christians apart from personal relationships of mutual recognition, along with respect for the personhood of the other. Correspondingly, the God of Christians cannot be understood apart from the personal, Trinitarian, interrelationship of the Father, Son, and Holy Spirit, People bearing the image of the relational God will be in relationship with one another, *analogia relationis*. They bear in relationship the image of the relational God. Further, these missional marks of the Christian church—its service (*diakonia*), its life together (*koinōnia*), and its witness (*martyria*)—cannot be understood fully apart from relationships, as deriving and occurring within relationships.

For example, *service* apart from *life together* tends toward patronizing acts of charity that create dependency, that do not honor an individual's or community's capacity, and that do not lead to sustainable development. Or, conversely, *life together* apart from the sense of responsible *service* tends toward a crisis of stewardship, blind to the opportunity to aggregate intentionally goods and services so that they might be extended to those in need. As Dietrich Bonhoeffer noted in a volume ironically called *Life Together*: "We are inclined to reply too quickly that the one real service to our neighbor is to serve them with the Word of God. It is true that there is no service that can equal this one. . . . Yet a Christian community does not consist solely of preachers of the Word."[3]

---

the Practice of Global Christianity and Intercultural Studies, Vera Blinn Chair at United Theological Seminary. See "The Processio-Missio Connection: A Starting Point in Missio Trinitatis or Overcoming the Immanent-Economic Divide in Missio Trinitatis," *Wesleyan Theological Journal* (October 2014).

3. Dietrich Bonhoeffer, *Life Together; Prayerbook of the Bible*, ed. Geffrey B. Kelly and trans. Daniel W. Bloesch and James H. Burtness, Dietrich Bonhoeffer Works 5 (Minneapolis: Fortress, 1996), 98.

A Historic Opportunity

The five-hundredth anniversary of the start of the Reformation, as the historian Jaroslav Pelikan once axiomatically observed, represents a "tragic necessity"[4] for all who confess Jesus Christ as Lord and are baptized into his death and resurrection. By "tragic," Pelikan was pointing to the ever-spiraling rupture of the church prompted by that first major breach—a problem some Protestants are quick to abet and slow to acknowledge (John 17:11); and by "necessity" he meant the historical moment's imperative to reassert, amid princes, powers, popes, and perversions of the gospel, God's saving gift of justification by grace—an urgency some Catholics do not immediately concede and some Eastern Orthodox consider irrelevant.

From a global, twenty-first-century perspective, however, this five-hundredth anniversary commemorates not merely a tragic necessity, but it also provides for Western Christians within Reformation traditions a historic opportunity; for Lutherans, in particular, the shifting demography of their membership suggests a momentous circumstance from which to reinvigorate their ecclesial and missional movement with gospel resources emanating from Lutheran traditions outside Europe and North America. Anniversaries are not only for looking backward, of course, but also provide occasions for looking forward. Moreover, for those who prioritize the church in mission, this five-hundredth anniversary can become an invitation to look within in order that we might look outward in a learning and listening posture toward the expanding global church.

---

4. Jaroslav Pelikan, *The Riddle of Roman Catholicism: Its History, Its Beliefs, Its Future* (London: Hodder and Stoughton, 1960).

Diakonia as Mercy or Service

The LCMS, since 2010, has promoted a threefold focus to thematize strategically its ministry. Derived from Scripture—the sole rule and norm for teaching in the LCMS—these dynamic foci are witness (*martyria*), mercy (*diakonia*), and life together (*koinōnia*), commonly abbreviated as WMLT. These ancient marks of the church reinforce the LCMS's confessional *fusion*, even as they catalyze a welcome missional *fission*. A church stabilized and united in confessional subscription (fusion) will walk together with clarity, confidence, and charity amid the inevitable disruptive messiness of being energetically in mission (fission).

WMLT provides, furthermore, a focused opportunity for theological conversation concerning the interpretation and implementation of these emphases. In that spirit, this chapter commends LCMS leaders for introducing WMLT even as it proposes that our current Reformation commemoration offers a momentous moment: as the LCMS embraces the opportunity to reimagine how WMLT can be more fully refined and defined by global expressions of its evangelical confession beyond North America and Europe, it could be anticipated that there might be a corresponding shift in the linguistic translation and theological conceptualization of *diakonia*: toward *service* rather than *mercy*.

First, the term "service" lends itself to fewer misunderstandings than "mercy" about the sort of compassionate interaction being undertaken, providing fewer semiotic misperceptions leading to condescension or paternalism—either among the beneficiaries (who internalize inferiority) or by the doers of *diakonia*.

The term "mercy" in the Christian understanding is never without divine dimensions reflected in one of the faith's oldest and purest prayers, *Kyrie eleison*. Mercy's effusive source is always God (Psalm 136). Humans, at best, serve as instruments providing others with gifts originating in God. Only in view of God's steadfast love (Rom. 12:2) do Christ-bearers offer themselves humbly in service to others. "Mercy" can carry a linguistic insistence on charitable action, conveying a relationship of power to powerlessness, of capacity to incapacity, of knowledge to lack of knowledge.

Ministries of compassion, relief, and support that are most effective, however, recognize the power, the capacity, and the knowledge resident within even the most debilitated communities. All people inherently possess agency (for working, for achieving potentially everything except salvation) since all people are created in God's image.

Finally, "mercy," as it is used in the English-speaking world, seems tinged with a tone of someone's benevolent disposition of forbearance toward another who is guilty of some moral transgression. Such discretionary withholding of punishment is akin in its usage to Jesus's biblical illustration of the Pharisee's smug petition as contrasted with the tax collector's urgent plea, "God, be merciful to me, a sinner!" (Luke 18:13).

The story of the father's lavish love, also known as the parable of the prodigal son, highlights the implication that those in need of mercy are experiencing their plight because of bad or sinful choices; as Arthur Just suggests rightly, the primary point is the "proclamation of the mercy of a loving father made manifest to the repentant sinner, no matter how gross the sinful conduct has been."[5] "Service" does not carry as readily that baggage or that judgment of the other. So, *diakonia* is most appositely translated as "service," striving to live out Luther's axiom that "there is no greater service of God than Christian love which helps and serves people living in poverty and need."[6]

When service is coupled missionally with life together and witness, it invites the sending community to see itself primarily engaged with prepositions of horizontality or companionship. So,

5. Arthur A. Just, *Luke 9:51–24:53*, *Concordia Commentary* (St. Louis: Concordia, 1997), 608.

6. Quoted in Carter Lindberg, *Beyond Charity: Reformation Initiatives for the Poor* (Minneapolis: Fortress, 1993), 164.

we are not in service *at* them or *for* them or *to* them, but we see ourselves related to them through the preposition "with." Such *with-ness*, especially with partner churches, implies mutual mission, partners joined by Christ (1 Cor. 12:12–27), "members of the same body, and sharers in the promise in Christ Jesus through the gospel" (Eph. 3:6).

Further, when witness, service, and life together are held together in creative tension, the level of sensitivity to contextual nuance will rise, as will the respect for everyday patterns, everyday speech, local customs and language—not imposed from above, but as Martin Luther suggested:

> We do not have to ask about the literal Latin or how we are to speak German. Rather we must ask the mother in the home, the children on the street, the common person in the market about this. We must be guided by their tongue, the manner of their speech, and do our translating accordingly. Then they will understand it and recognize that we are speaking German to them. . . . The literal Latin is a great barrier to speaking proper German.[7]

Learning from Ethiopia

The conference was called "*Diakonia*." It was held in Adidas Ababa, Ethiopia, in 2010. I attended it as president and CEO of Lutheran World Relief. During a break in the sessions I was privileged to sit with the president of the EECMY, Iteffa Gobena. This church body had grown from 65,000 members at its founding in 1959 to more than 5 million members in 2010. As of 2015 it hovered at the 7 million mark in membership. In light of the struggle for baptisms

---

7. Martin Luther, "An Open Letter on Translating," September 15, 1530 (LW 35:189).

and confirmations in the LCMS, I took the opportunity to hear and learn about the Holy Spirit's work in that communion. Gobena identified four reasons for this growth:

1. "We emphasize equipping the saints and the ministry of the laity." All baptized believers are called into action for the work of ministry. The exercise of spiritual gifts belongs to the whole church, not just the ordained clergy; in fact, the EECMY has a dire shortage of clergy, but this has not hindered its growth because of its equipping of the saints.

2. "We've been in revival since we were founded." I worshiped with them; the character of their liturgy is ebullient with joy and evangelistic energy. Despite the barren, spare, simple outdoor churches, multiple times there were baptisms. More than spiritual fervor, revival refers to repentance and baptismal renewal.

3. "We are in mission to the whole person." Again, there is nothing particularly innovative about this emphasis. The church operates a vast network of social service, healthcare, and outreach ministries within the nation of Ethiopia and beyond—especially among some of the most marginalized people groups. In their strong commitment to ministries of service, this church is teaching us all that witness and life together become disingenuous without care for the livelihood of others, especially those with whom one shares fellowship.

4. "We are prepared to die for our faith." Some in their church body rendered the ultimate sacrifice. In Chapter 4 above, we spoke of Gudina Tumsa, who served as the general secretary of the EECMY in the 1970s. Because he refused to submit to the demands of the revolutionary Marxist military government seeking to silence the church, he was arrested and tortured. After he was released, he could have fled from Ethiopia while he had the chance, but, like Dietrich Bonhoeffer in Nazi Germany, he refused to do so. He was re-arrested and viciously murdered. Gudina Tumsa firmly believed that God's justice in the world and God's justifying act in Christ are inextricably linked. He wrote:

"The Gospel of Jesus Christ is God's power to save everyone who believes it. . . . It is too powerful to be compromised by any social or political system."[8] The life of Gudina was resonant with that of another early African church leader, Tertullian, who affirmed that "the blood of the martyrs is the seed of the Church" (*Apologeticus*, chapter 50). He should be remembered among us (*Augsburg Confession* XXI) and the day of his death, July 28, should be commemorated.

Life Together and Diversity

The church's life together requires constant vigilance against any one particular cultural expression becoming an exclusive unifier, filtering out of the fellowship those who are different. Life together means being unified in Christ, with a common confession of faith, as agents of Christ through witness and service.[9]

The sole source of life (*bios*) and meaningful existence is God's

8. Tumsa, "The Role of a Christian," 200–204. See also Tumsa's "Memorandum to Ato Emmanuel Abraham," 271–79.

9. While it is not a sin to move in homogenous circles, it is a sin not to recognize one's neighbor. It is the essence of sin to live a radically inward-turned life. It is a sin, under the guise of natural self-limitation, to ignore or exclude or oppress others who are trying to gain entrance to opportunity or membership or contracts through a rigid affiliation to one's networks of friendly association (see Luther's explanation of the ninth and tenth commandments). The church is not a social club; it is a society of the redeemed, joined to Jesus Christ by baptism first and foremost, not by a group's cultural identity. Lutherans have been guilty, in my estimation, of equating their Lutheran-ness with an inward-focused Garrison Keillor–esque identity. This exclusivizing tendency in Lutheranism, where expressions of Nordic and Germanic identity—music, being literate, art, style, even humor—are almost tantamount with the gospel, has largely contributed to our overwhelming whiteness and English-speaking character. The Mormons, who until the 1970s had laws against minorities having full membership, are *three times* as diverse as we are. It irks me that we say we are knitted together primarily by our Confession of Doctrine when that does not seem to be the case.

creative, redeeming, and enlightening Word to the world. This life is: replete with dignity (*Würde*)[10] and purpose (*zōē*, John 10:10); rich with integrity; redolent with living traditions robust enough to both anchor community and prompt spiritual growth; and rooted in the fellowship of Christ's forgiveness. "If human dignity, as built in the image of God, ceases to be based in God's address to human beings, which extends without exception to all humans and awards them a principal authorization to live, other criteria will gain prevalence."[11] These "other criteria" might include cultural or sociological phenomena. When an individual's or a group's fundamental identity becomes incurved (*incurvatio in seipsum*), turning only to their own needs, rather than oriented toward Christ and neighbor, people are prone, according to Luther, to make false gods even of otherwise virtuous goods: "great learning, wisdom, power, prestige, family and honor."[12]

These pursuits—apart from God, apart from the deliverance of Jesus Christ, apart from the Holy Spirit's enlightenment—become idols. These prizes and gifts, apart from their being subsumed to the worship (*leitourgia*) of God's Son, become idolized. This happens quite apart from any inkling of deliberate, conscious intention since such desiring "sticks and clings to our nature all the way to the grave," according to Luther.[13]

Not only do these priorities in themselves not sustain and nurture the sort of life in which God intends us to live, but "great learning, wisdom, power, prestige, family and honor" by the very vigor of their virtue become invisible fences that exclude those lacking "great learning, wisdom, power, prestige, family and honor" and

10. Michael Rosen notes that, rightly or wrongly, Immanuel Kant's thought about dignity occupies a critical philosophical centerpiece of any discussion of dignity: "The German word for dignity [is] closely related etymologically to *Wert*, the term for 'worth or value'" (*Dignity*, 19).

11. Schwanke, "Luther's Theology of Creation," 205.

12. Martin Luther, *Large Catechism* (*BC*, 387).

13. Martin Luther, *Large Catechism* (*BC*, 387).

prevent *koinōnia*. Without the tempering effect of a spirituality of stewardship, the ego will create a God from the good. Without the incursion of outsiders, strangers, and new neighbors, redemptive truth often is not received.

Remarkably, Jesus is recognized in Mark's Gospel by the "way he breathed his last." This recognition did not come from a sacred insider, or a tribe-member, or a disciple, but from a secular outsider, an agent of the state, an imperial mercenary. At Jesus's maximal point of godforsaken suffering, it takes *an other* to tell the truth *on the same*.[14]

But the mere position of being an outsider does not ensure truth. Lack of proximity and familiarity can lead to exoticizing and fetishizing the other. For example, during the development of the African American worship supplement in the 1990s, another well-intended impulse—that of fascination with the other—led to a sort of liturgical dilettantism evidenced in the introduction of rarefied practices that, albeit pondered in academic theology and mused about at conferences, were and are not recognized in the worship customs of the vast majority of everyday African Americans.

One such practice proposed by more liberal Lutherans included libation rituals, a traditional heritage ritual among some West Africans, which were debated for hours though they are virtually unknown among black Lutherans or committee members from "real" congregations who were suspicious of the wisdom of their introduction. Furthermore, very few Lutheran Christians who are Africans from the continent followed these practices.

Moving beyond Either/Or

Gudina Tumsa highlighted in his Nairobi address (1974) "the contrast between the traditional African concept of life and the West-

---

14. John D. Caputo, *What Would Jesus Deconstruct? The Good News of Post-modernism for the Church* (Grand Rapids: Baker Academic, 2007), 29.

ern concept."[15] To heal, for example, is not simply a question of medical care, but "has to do with the restoration of man to liberty and wholeness": "In the ministry of Jesus we note that forgiveness of sins and healing of the body, feeding the hungry and spiritual nurture, opposing de-humanizing structures and identifying himself with the weak were never at any time divided or departmentalized. He saw man as a whole and was always ready to give help where the need was most obvious." The theology and practice of this comprehensive approach leads us to an amplification of the notion concerning salvation. Jesus saves from sin, from malaria, and from oppression.

Typical dichotomizing is not only unhelpful, but untrue: either service or verbal witness, either social justice or moral righteousness, either prophetic zeal or charismatic spiritual zeal are false and unnecessary options. In their engagement with the rest of the Christian world, Christians in the West bear a unique challenge to be critically confessional and self-critical, and to be reflectively creative in mutual mission. The relationality implicit in a *missio trinitatis* approach will help cultivate greater unity as the church lives in witness, service, and life together.

15. Gudina Tumsa, "Serving the Whole Man: A Responsible Church Ministry and Flexible International Aid Relationship," in *Proclamation and Human Development. LWF Documentation from a Lutheran World Federation Consultation in Nairobi, Kenya, October 21-25, 1974* (Geneva: Lutheran World Federation, 1974).

CHAPTER 7

The *Koinōnia* of the Justified

Toward an Eschatology of Faith

In 1987, I received a scathing letter from a pastor's widow in response to one of my published devotions reflecting on Holy Communion in light of Luther's understanding of *koinōnia*. My comments were made based on Luther's sermon "The Blessed Sacrament of the Holy and True Body of Christ, and the Brotherhoods" (1519).[1] I wrote this devotion for the Advent and Christmas seasons, reflecting on the wonderful presence of the incarnate Christ in bread and wine for us. I emphasized this gift of Christ for the forgiveness of our sins and for our binding together as Christ's community of faith. This woman took particular offense to my rephrasing of this quote from Luther's sermon: "In this sacrament, therefore, man is given through the priest a sure sign from God himself that he is thus united with Christ and his saints and has all things in common [with them], that Christ's sufferings and life are his own, together with the lives and sufferings of all the saints."[2] She insisted on Christ's real presence in the sacrament for the sole purpose of the forgiveness of her sins. She also practically called me an apostate for suggesting that through Christ's union in Holy Communion, we are also united

1. *LW* 35:49–78.
2. *LW* 35:52.

with our sisters and brothers in a real union, a communion with each other, which compels us to care for and serve each other no matter who we are.

Not wanting to engage in a back-and-forth argument with this sister in Christ, I called her pastor. (After all, I am sure that this faithful lady, like many Grandma Smiths, has contributed to help the poor with the little they have.) I explained to her pastor the situation and the issue at hand. We are called, I underscored, in Luther's reading of 1 Corinthians 10–12 to a real binding communion with one another because we are united in Christ's real presence. We cannot affirm a real presence of Christ with us and for us in Holy Communion, unless we affirm a real binding union to serve one another as Christ's church. We are God's church because we are truly and really united in Christ. To my dismay he also took issue with me. He doubted my words. He asked for solid proof. I ended up sending him a copy of Luther's sermon. I followed up with some telephone conversations. I was talking to a pastor who had been educated at a Lutheran seminary. Lutheran pastors happen (or are supposed) to also be sacramental priests who affirm the communion, the *koinōnia*, that we have in Christ through the sacraments of Holy Communion and baptism. This *koinōnia* is crucial to our confession of the evangelical catholic faith.

Luther provides a clear definition of *koinōnia* in his sermon on "The Blessed Sacrament," following the teachings present in 1 Corinthians:

> The significance or effect of this sacrament is fellowship of all the saints. From this it derives its common name *synaxis* [Greek] or *communio* [Latin], that is, fellowship. And the Latin *communicare* [commune or communicate] or as we say in German, *zum Sacrament gehen* [go to the sacrament] means to take part in the fellowship. Hence it is that Christ and all saints are one spiritual body, just as the inhabitants of a city are one

community and one body, each citizen being a member of the other and of the entire city.[3]

In terms of North American evangelical theology the preference for the Reformation is one where Luther's existential angst is right up front and center. The personal relationship with Christ is the most important element of one's faith life. The sense of our *koinōnia* in Christ is not a central and critical issue for the faith. I have also found this to be the case in most of Latino evangelical and Pentecostal churches. Salvation has to do with a personal faith and the church, the *koinōnia* of believers, does not really play an essential role in their faith life.[4] But they are not alone. I have also found many mainline Anglo as well as Latino sacramental churches in which the true unity that we have in our *convivir*, life together, in Christ is not fully actively proclaimed and lived. This anemic understanding of ecclesiology needs to be addressed in light of two important factors. The first is that in reading the Bible in Spanish, the text clearly points out that Christ, as the center of God's Trinitarian mission, is always creating a *koinōnia*, a life together, a *convivir*, of God's people in his union with the whole community of faith. Second, there is present in the Latino festive life a sense of *convivir* (life together) in church, family, and society. These points of departure, however, need further reimagining to strengthen our *koinōnia* in order to carry out God's mission. They need to be addressed from the perspective of an eschatology of faith from the margins.

---

3. *LW* 35:50–51.

4. See Justo L. González, "In Quest of a Protestant Hispanic Ecclesiology," in *Teología en Conjunto: A Collaborative Hispanic Protestant Theology*, ed. José David Rodríguez and Loida I. Martell-Otero (Louisville: Westminster John Knox, 1997), 80–83. González traces several reasons for this state of affairs. The end result has been a weak or nonexistent ecclesiology among most Latino evangelical and Pentecostal churches.

Reading 1 Corinthians from the Margins

During the past few decades, the ecclesiology of *koinōnia* has been at the center of ecumenical dialogue among Catholics, Lutherans, Anglicans, and many other denominations. Pope Benedict XVI claimed that communion ecclesiology was the very heart and distinctive teaching of Vatican II concerning the church. Pope John Paul II, his predecessor, had already declared the importance of this envisioned and practiced unity in his encyclical *Ut Unum Sint* (That All May Be One), which came to light on May 25, 1995. This encyclical is grounded in Jesus's priestly prayer in John 17, pinpointing verse 11 in Latin from the Vulgate: *ut unum sint*. Carl Braaten rightly observes how Pope John Paul II highlights the robust Trinitarian missiological emphasis of this prayer for the sake of seeking unity.[5] Gary Riebe-Estrella underscores how important this vision is in *Lumen Gentium* (no. 1), the Vatican II Constitution on the Church, for the church must "mirror the reality of being a family as God envisions."[6] Pope John Paul II sought in his encyclical a communion, *koinōnia*, with all Christian churches for the sake of proclaiming and living the Trinitarian mission of God in our times. There is no doubt, as he and other ecumenical theologians have observed, that the priestly prayer in John 17 seeks this unity. This unity must be sought for the sake of the mission and witness of the church.[7] I believe that the Pauline apostolic blessing in 2 Corinthians 13:13 affirms the priestly prayer's yearning in John 17:11. Our *koinōnia*

5. Carl Braaten, *That All May Believe: A Theology of the Gospel and the Mission of the Church* (Grand Rapids: Eerdmans, 2008), 47, 57–58. Cf. *Ut Unum Sint* (no. 27) (http://w2.vatican.va/content/john-paul-ii/en/encyclicals/documents/hf_jp-ii_enc_25051995_ut-unum-sint.html).

6. Gary Riebe-Estrella, "Pueblo and Church," in *From the Heart of Our People: Latino/a Explorations of Catholic Systematic Theology*, ed. Orlando O. Espín and Miguel H. Díaz (Maryknoll, NY: Orbis, 1999), 183.

7. This Trinitarian binding is affirmed in *Lumen Gentium* (no. 1), the Vatican II document on the church.

is to be created in the Trinitarian presence of God's gifts of grace and love.

This chapter conforms to this vision. Its methodology, though, is from below and not from above. There is great validity for our times in Pope John Paul II's proposals in *Ut Unum Sint,* and they need to be considered. However, they need to be considered first by listening to the people's voices from the margins and not the ecclesiastical concerns of the church as an institution, whether Catholic, Protestant, evangelical, or any other kind of Christian brand. In fact, Pope John Paul II and his successor, Pope Benedict XVI, attempted to silence the voices of liberation theologians, such as Leonardo Boff, when they cried out in their writings for a church from below, a church from the poor and the margins.[8] In other words, the papal efforts toward ecumenicity have been in the recent past marred by abusive authority from above. We should be thankful for the recent efforts of many churches, in particular the courageous efforts put forward in life and spirit by Pope Francis, to listen to the margins in pursuing a living *koinōnia.* Nevertheless, this listening needs to engage in a more radical reimagining. The seeking of a living *koinōnia* is more often than not bogged down within the various church hierarchical structures, which seek to promote their institution and their particular brand of Christianity. These efforts, even when institutional concerns are set aside, lose their vitality when the *koinōnia* of the church is sought only through a "mystical union" that neglects the incarnational implications of this union. Therefore, this requires that we engage in more than listening.

---

8. See Leonardo Boff, *Church, Charism and Power,* trans. John W. Diercksmeier (New York: Crossroad, 1981). Boff infuriated Popes John Paul II and Benedict XVI because of his ecclesiastical view of the church grounded from below by the presence of the Holy Spirit among the poor and within the margins. He was submitted to a process under the Sacred Congregation of the Faith in 1984 for this posture. Cardinal Ratzinger, who became Pope Benedict XVI, was the director of the Congregation, as well as one of Boff's past thesis advisors. Boff was silenced for this posture (see Alberto L. García, "Leonardo Boff," in *The Encyclopedia of Christian Civilization,* ed. George Thomas Kurian [Sussex: Wiley-Blackwell, 2011], 1:287-90).

It requires a shift in our modus operandi from below in seeking communion. This is what I perceive that 1 and 2 Corinthians allow us to do. These letters provide the key points for this shift.

Joseph Mangina's essay "The Cross-Shaped Church: A Pauline Amendment to the Ecclesiology of Koinōnia" underscores how important 1 and 2 Corinthians are in constructing a communion ecclesiology for our times. Mangina, as well as many other Protestants, evangelicals, and Catholics, finds that communion ecclesiology is one of the crucial issues for all churches in our times.[9] A reimagining of the Reformation for our times is unimaginable without addressing this issue head-on.

Mangina's central thesis is that "ecclesial *koinōnia* can only be cruciform, and that if it lacks this character it cannot be the *koinōnia* of [God's] Son, Jesus Christ our Lord (1 Cor. 1:9)."[10] Mangina, like Luther, underscores that there cannot be a *koinōnia* of the faithful apart from submitting ourselves together to Christ's cruciform presence among us. Mangina finds this cruciform existence as the guiding light in Paul's teaching on spiritual gifts.[11] The usual teaching on spiritual gifts by many evangelical and Protestant groups is that these gifts are complementary. Therefore, in this way of thinking, it is understood that all Christians possess these gifts of the Spirit for the sole purpose of building the "church"—the church being in this context usually interpreted as some form of witnessing machine or body. But this is far from Paul's key teaching concerning *koinōnia* and spiritual gifts. It means rather that the stronger members must identify with the weaker members. It means that we must affirm their validity within the body of Christ. It means that we must refrain from exercising our own rights if it means offending or hurting a brother or a sister.

---

9. See Joseph L. Mangina, "The Cross-Shaped Church: A Pauline Amendment to the Ecclesiology of Koinonia," in *Critical Issues in Ecclesiology*, ed. Alberto L. García and Susan K. Wood (Grand Rapids: Eerdmans, 2011), 68–87. There are several authors who address the issue of communion ecclesiology in this book.

10. Mangina, "The Cross-Shaped Church," 71.

11. Mangina, "The Cross-Shaped Church," 70.

Mangina follows in essence Luther's interpretation concerning the exercise of spiritual gifts in the sermon cited above. In pursuing this vision of *koinōnia* there is a cruciform existence that binds our living together. We are bound by this gift from God to act in this manner.

> This fellowship consists in this, that all the spiritual possessions of Christ and his saints are shared with and become the common property of him who receives this sacrament. Again all sufferings and sins also become common property; and thus love engenders love in return and [mutual love] unites. To carry out our homely figure, it is like a city where every citizen shares with all the others the city's name, honor, freedom . . . while at the same time he shares all the dangers of fire and flood, enemies and death . . . and the like. For he who would share in the profits must also share in the costs, and ever recompense love with love. Here we see that whoever injures one citizen injures an entire city and all its citizens; whoever benefits one [citizen] deserves favor and thanks from all the others. So also in our natural body, as St. Paul says in I Corinthians 12 [vv. 25–26], where he gives this sacrament a spiritual explanation, "The members have [the same] care for one another; if one member suffers, all suffer together; if one member is honored, all rejoice together." This is obvious: if anyone's foot hurts him, yes, even the little toe, the eye at once looks at it, the fingers grasp it, the face puckers, the whole body bends over to it, and all are concerned with this small member; again, once it is cared for all the other members are benefited. This comparison must be noted well if one wishes to understand this sacrament.[12]

Luther takes note in an implicit manner that *koinōnia* must also be lived in public spaces. Societies as well as the church are important spaces to demonstrate the presence of God. The weak and

12. *LW* 35:51–52.

despised, those in the margins, must not be humiliated but honored whether in our church or in our city. Not to do so is to limit God to one's sphere or place. It also hinders the witness of the gospel in the world. We must be open, therefore, to share all those spaces as God's sacred spaces because we understand our *koinōnia* in Christ also impacts God's presence in the world. This can be further understood by reading 1 Corinthians from the margins.

A key and crucial text for Luther's understanding of the theology of the cross is found in 1 Corinthians 1. This text is at the center of Luther's reflection on Thesis 20 during the Heidelberg Disputation in 1518.[13] Paul proclaims: "For the message about the cross is foolishness to those who are perishing, but to us who are being saved it is the power of God" (v. 18). Paul is speaking here to an international community made up of Jews and Gentiles. God shatters human wisdom, reason, of the "philosophers of this age" who use it for their own purposes rather than to glorify God. He also shatters the pretense of those who claim to be God's privileged people because they are particularly blessed with God's miraculous signs and power (vv. 20-24). Paul is proclaiming here God's justification for us. God shatters our human pretense, our idolatry, and calls us into a new righteousness to be his people. God declares us worthy human beings and calls us to be his own in Christ.

However, Paul's proclamation of the cross is not a call to righteousness made to only benefit individually each person in the community or to benefit one particular group over another group within the community (vv. 10-17). It is an incarnational call made to a community and for the sake of this community. It is, therefore, a call that cannot be had or lived out outside a cruciform *koinōnia* with Christ and the people of God (v. 17; 1 Cor. 10:15-17). Many Lutherans and other Christians have attempted to separate these two important dimensions concerning redemption. In fact, Luther does

13. *LW* 31:52-53. See also Thesis 22, where Luther reflects further on this malady when human beings search for personal glory (53-54).

not emphasize the place and role of the cross for the *koinōnia* of believers as he explains Thesis 20. This was not, after all, the question at hand. Therefore, Thesis 20 could be misunderstood in terms of a very individualistic understanding of salvation. According to Luther and Paul, individuals are called by faith through grace in Christ to be children of God. But there is much more. This call is given at our baptism to become the people of God. This is very much present for Luther and Paul in their affirmation of the Lord's Supper.

As we have read above, Luther understands, as his reading of 1 Corinthians points out, that we must live out our *koinōnia* and our salvation in terms of the Eucharist. This reality must be lived out and expressed, in Luther's reading of 1 Corinthians 12, by exercising our spiritual gifts in solidarity with the weak and marginalized. But it is more than serving their physical needs. This is a point that Mangina stresses in his essay: it also means refraining from exercising our own rights if doing so offends a brother or a sister. It also means that all members of the community deserve the same care and respect, even the ones considered less significant (vv. 14–26).[14] In terms of Latino communities it means valuing their identity within the community. We need to read 1 Corinthians 10–12 in light of this point of departure.

Paul's writings to the church in Corinth are significant for our task at hand. First Corinthians is particularly important because it is considered by many New Testament scholars to contain the earliest account of the church's celebration of the Lord's Supper and the words that Jesus used for this celebration. First Corinthians 15 also contains the earliest account of the resurrection and its impact on the early church.[15] First Corinthians also reveals a great deal

---

14. Mangina, "The Cross-Shaped Church," 70.

15. Justo L. González, *Faith and Wealth: A History of Early Christian Ideas on the Origin, Significance, and Use of Money* (Eugene, OR: Wipf and Stock, 2002), 82–85. See also Gerd Theissen, *The Social Setting of Pauline Christianity: Essays on Corinth* (Philadelphia: Fortress, 1982), and Wayne Meeks, *The Social World of the Apostle Paul* (New Haven: Yale University Press, 1983).

about the critical issues and dynamics of the early New Testament church. It was written to a divided church made up of people from different ethnic groups, poor and rich alike. The church at Corinth was, however, made up mainly of converts from the city's lower economic and social groups. This created great challenges to the fellowship. Paul's exhortation is loud and clear in the opening statements of his first letter: "God is faithful; by him you were called into the fellowship [*koinōnia*] of his Son, Jesus Christ our Lord" (1 Cor. 1:9). He calls the Corinthians in this light to exercise their spiritual gifts, setting their sights on an eschatological, in fact apocalyptic, hope awaiting God's completion (1:7). The climax and epicenter of this letter is the living *koinōnia* created by our common bond in the Lord's table, the Eucharist. It is a *koinōnia* from below in communion with Christ rather than a superimposed hierarchical *koinōnia* that takes place only as the church dictates. This is why we meditate now on 1 Corinthians 11:23–26 from the margins.

For I received from the Lord what I also handed on to you [*ustedes*], that the Lord Jesus on the night when he was betrayed took a loaf of bread, and when he had given thanks, he broke it and said, "This is my body that is for you [*ustedes*]. Do this [*hagan esto*] in remembrance of me." In the same way he took the cup also, after supper, saying, "This cup is the new covenant in my blood. Do this [*hagan esto*], as often as you drink [*beban*] it, in remembrance of me." For as often as you eat [*coman*] this bread and drink [*beban*] the cup, you proclaim [*proclaman*] the Lord's death until he comes.[16]

16. It reads in Spanish: "Yo recibí del Señor lo mismo que les he enseñado a ustedes: Que la noche que fue entregado, el Señor Jesús tomó pan; y luego de dar gracias, lo partió, y dijo: 'Tomen, coman; esto es mi cuerpo que por ustedes es partido; hagan esto en mí memoria.' Asimismo también después de haber cenado tomó la copa y dijó: 'Esta copa es el nuevo pacto en mi sangre; hagan esto todas las veces que la beban, en memoria de mí.' Por lo tanto, todas las veces que coman este pan y beban esta copa, proclaman la muerte del Señor a hasta que él venga" (RV, 2009).

When Latinos read these words in Spanish they are able to see that Holy Communion is always a communal act. This is what the New Testament Greek text also clearly explains. Our reading of the text in English does not point this out. The Spanish text is clear. The bread is "my body that is given for you [*ustedes* = second-person plural]." The cup is given for you to drink together (*beban* = second-person plural). This act of eating and drinking, the "do this" (*hagan esto* = second-person plural imperative), is an urgent command given to God's people in community. The final and most important goal in all this is "you proclaim [*proclaman* = second-person plural active indicative]." That is, you, as the community of faith sharing Christ's body, continue proclaiming together Christ's death and resurrection on our behalf. It is clear that the Eucharist is a communal act. It is a real and effective *koinōnia*, a sharing of Christ's death and life for us.

Paul already clarifies this in 1 Corinthians 10:16-17: "The cup of blessing that we bless, is it not a sharing [*la comunión* = *koinōnia*] in the blood of Christ? The bread that we break, is it not a sharing [*la comunión* = *koinōnia*] in the body of Christ? Because there is one bread, we who are many are one body, for we all partake [*metéxomen*, active, indicative] of the one bread." The partaking in verse 17 is synonymous with the *koinōnia* acts in verse 16. This text also resonates in Latino communities when it is read in light of its cultural significance.

We cannot ignore Paul's reason for writing these words in 1 Corinthians 10 and 11. It is of utmost importance in affirming our life together in the margins. In the sixteenth century and even before, and to this day, a great many Catholic and Protestant theologians have primarily engaged in a rationalistic discerning of the text above or consider the Eucharist a mere appendage to the gospel.[17] Luther, however, as Jaroslav Pelikan observes and I concur through

17. See Jaroslav Pelikan, *The Christian Tradition: A History of the Development of Doctrine* (Chicago: University of Chicago Press, 1984), 4:52–59, 158–61, 176–77, 189–92. The Zürich Consensus (1549), interpreting Calvin and Bullinger on the sacraments, states: "the sacraments are appendages [appendices] of the gospel" (189).

my readings of Luther, "insisted that he was not basing his belief in the words 'This is my body' on a rationalistic hypothesis, but on the word and promise of Christ."[18] Luther offers a clear answer to this when Zwingli wants to evoke a rationalistic answer from him concerning the presence of the body of Christ. Luther clarifies for Zwingli what he really meant when he wrote with chalk on the table "Hoc est corpus meum" ("This is my body"). Luther states at the colloquy at Marburg that "I have simply quoted the words of Christ. . . . I have nothing to do with mathematical reasons, and I exclude or reject completely from the Lord's Supper the adverb of space. The words are 'this is my body,' not 'there is my body.'"[19]

However, in practice, many Lutherans in effect end up following a rationalistic practice by localizing the real presence in the bread and wine for the only purpose that a believer eats and drinks for herself or himself. The end result is that the critical dimension of the presence of Christ to bind the Christian community is ignored or totally absent. This occurs mainly when theologians do not wish to emphasize Luther's central reading of this sacrament as *communio*, a *koinōnia* with the body of Christ.[20] First Corinthians

18. Pelikan, *The Christian Tradition*, 4:160.

19. See Basil Hall, "*Hoc est corpus meum*: The Centrality of the Real Presence for Luther," in *Luther: Theologian for Catholics and Protestants*, ed. George Hule (Edinburgh: T&T Clark, 1985), 138.

20. See Hall, "*Hoc est corpus meum*," 120-21. Hall believes that Luther's sermon to "the Brotherhoods" in 1529 is not the proper place to start in discerning his teaching on the Lord's Supper. Hall believes that this sermon in fact does not do justice to Luther's first and foremost emphasis on Holy Communion, which is "the objective givenness of this sacrament" under the Word (120). This starting point, in my opinion, derails the centrality of the sacrament as *koinōnia*. It is true that Luther dedicates great time and effort in other writings to explain that participating in the body of Christ is not just a representative or memorial act (such as in his treatise *This Is My Body* [1557] [*LW* 37:3–150]). However, in other writings, such as *Confession of the Lord's Supper*, when Luther engages the issue of *koinōnia* in 1 Corinthians 10:16–17, he is more preoccupied in addressing the issue of the Christian participating, communing with the "body of Christ," versus a memorial or representative eating (*LW* 37:339–60).

10 and 11 critically teaches our binding together and serving each other because of the *koinōnia* we share in Christ.[21] Luther's spirit and wisdom in interpreting 1 Corinthians 11 can address the situation that Latinos and Latinas are facing in their church contexts and situations today because it binds them to the way of the cross in Jesus's life. Eliseo Pérez Álvarez offers similar insights in his essay "In Memory of Me: A Hispanic/Latino Christology beyond Borders."[22] He observes: "It is my conviction that this sacrament [the Eucharist] provides a meaningful correlation between the life and ministry of Jesus Christ and our Hispanic/Latino experience."[23] The Eucharist compels us to remember how Jesus lived out *koinōnia* with his people. It is a cruciform *koinōnia*. Jesus gives himself so we may have an abundant life together. We remember Jesus's way of the cross as his ultimate sacrifice for us. We remember in the Eucharist Jesus's ongoing risen presence calling us in this festive *koinōnia* to be a new people of God. It is in this affirmation and remembrance that we can engage the important issue of identity. This is the most critical issue to address in order for Christ's *koinōnia* to bear fruit in the Latino communities.

The term *koinōnia* was employed readily in New Testament times to mean partnership in business. It is noted, for example, that the sons of Zebedee were *koinōnoi* with Peter in Luke 5:10.[24] They had a business partnership. Acts 2:42-47 clarifies that this participation, *koinōnia*, involved a sharing that was not only spiritual but also material. This sharing was a concrete *convivir* (life together) in which the early Christians opened their homes and shared with one

---

21. In essence, we need to rephrase and apply the Lutheran distinctive emphasis on the ubiquity of Christ to *koinōnia*: "finitum est capax infinitae communionis Christi" (the finite is capable of sharing Christ's infinite *koinōnia*)—because of the real presence!

22. Eliseo Pérez Álvarez, "In Memory of Me: A Hispanic/Latino Christology beyond Borders," in *Teología en Conjunto*, 33-49.

23. Álvarez, "In Memory of Me," 33.

24. See Justo L. González, *Faith and Wealth*, 83.

another God's consolation and their daily bread.[25] Sometimes this text is set aside by contemporary Christians because it seems to call for an extreme form of *koinōnia*, or "communism" as it is sometimes referred to in pejorative terms. Justo González in *Faith and Wealth* describes how this is not necessarily the case. This has to do with a misinterpretation of the text.

The early church, in spite of not being an idyllic community and committing many sins and errors, focused on an ongoing *koinōnia*. Acts 2:45 is sometimes misread.[26] It is not that the believers sold all their goods hook, line, and sinker. The text reads: "And they were selling [imperfect tense] their possessions and belongings and distributing [imperfect tense] the proceeds to all, as any had need" (ESV).[27] The practice was, as the use of the imperfect tense in Greek suggests, an ongoing sharing to meet the needs of the community. Paul, in spite of the frictions between poor and rich, continues to urge the church to live in this incarnate *koinōnia* for the sake of the less fortunate (1 Cor. 16:1-4; 2 Cor. 8:13-20; 9:5-7). But this living, active *koinōnia* means more than the sharing of our goods with the less fortunate in the context of 1 Corinthians 11. We are called to be a new people centered in an eschatological hope. This hope and expectation needs to be remembered and lived out through the sharing of Christ's body and blood.

Paul is not, therefore, admonishing the wealthy for being wealthy but rather for not engaging in a cruciform *koinōnia*. The practice during those days was to engage in an *agapē* meal at home churches, a sharing and breaking of bread, before concluding with the supreme act of *koinōnia*, the sharing in the body and blood of Christ with one another. The Eucharist had to be celebrated as a fes-

---

25. This is what Paul in fact exhorts the community of faith to do as he opens 2 Corinthians (1:3-7) with an unusual doxology.

26. James 2:14-17 is a clear reminder of this neglect in the practice of a concrete *koinōnia* by the rich toward the poor in Jerusalem. James exhorts them to wake up from their selfishness.

27. Justo L. González, *Faith and Wealth*, 82.

tive event of present eschatological possibilities where the last (the marginal community) would be invited to occupy the first seats in this celebration. The marginal members had to be valued and honored as integral members of that community. What they said and did had to matter. *Koinōnia* occurred when the individuals, even the apostles, relinquished their status for the sake of this living community in Christ (Matt. 20:1–16, 20–28; 1 Cor. 12:22–31).[28] This had to be an ongoing practice within their eschatological festive hope.

The people of God found their identity and meaning in this *convivir*, life together, in the sacramental action of receiving and giving God's gift of life. This action meant the celebration of Christ's final banquet as a real present possibility. Their accomplishments or monetary richness were not to be the building blocks of their identity as God's people. These had to be set aside, abrogated, for the sake of the community. The people's identity was forged in their *convivir*, life together, in the Eucharistic life. They were celebrating in essence God's festive hope. Paul grounds this *convivir*, time and time again, in a sacramental life, bound not only by the blood and body of Christ but also by the same Spirit given in our baptism, enabling us to become one body (1 Cor. 12:12–13). It is a cruciform celebration. This outpouring of the Spirit is in essence also a sign of God's festive hope. This eschatological hope binds as worthy members of the *koinōnia* those considered less and inferior within the community of faith (Luke 4:14–19; Acts 2:16–20). What does this mean for US Latino communities?

Koinōnia as Festive Hope

A reflection on ecclesiology among US Latino evangelicals and Protestants is practically nonexistent. There are some encouraging

---

28. This does not mean that they relinquished their office but rather that they honored and valued the cruciform discipleship of the community of faith and they also engaged in a servant communal leadership among them (see 1 Cor. 12:22–31).

first steps being taken among US Catholic Latino theologians on ecclesiology.[29] This is ironic since living in a community, particularly the extended family, is what forges the identity of Latinos and Latinas.[30] Persons primarily form their identities in mainstream American culture through a process of individuation. They distance themselves from the group to find who they are. They give more credence to the "American Dream," that is, how much they have accomplished as individuals in society, in defining their human worth. A case in point is when my wife and I took our daughter Yvette to settle for the first time in college. The mother of her new roommate wanted to know right away what I did for a living. She wanted to know how accomplished I was. I was more interested in her family. I wanted to know where she came from, how many siblings she had, and the like. Most Latinos are aware that our identities are born through a mutual interplay of obligations, rights, and privileges that benefit individuals because it benefits our living together as a family and a community. Speaking of our salvation, what makes us whole is unthinkable outside our bond in community. We need to explore now how this plays out in different venues within Latino communities. The focal locus for our inquiry will be the predominant theme of "fiesta" within the everyday life and rituals of Latinos.

The history of Latinos in the United States is primarily one of cultural rather than economic oppression. Latino theologians, therefore, begin at a different point of departure from that of Leonardo Boff to affirm an ecclesiology from below. Most Latinos in the United States find themselves as a pilgrim people. This is also the case for a great many second- and third-generation Latinos. A *koinōnia* from the margins within US Latino communities takes

---

29. Orlando E. Espín, ed., *Building Bridges, Doing Justice: Constructing a Latino/a Ecumenical Theology* (Maryknoll, NY: Orbis, 2009).

30. See Riebe-Estrella, "Pueblo and Church," 172–76; Roberto S. Goizueta, "Nosotros: Community as the Birthplace of the Self," chapter 3 in *Caminemos con Jesús: Toward a Hispanic/Latino Theology of Accompaniment* (Maryknoll, NY: Orbis, 1995), 47–56.

note of the walls that have been created preventing Latinos from being fully accepted as worthy and contributing members to the entire community in the United States. This has created deep wounds and alienation in our identity as human beings.[31] This is also evident within Christian denominations, and even within many independent Christian churches.

As already stated, we Latinos are who we are because we are welcomed as integral and valuable members of our community. Our existence in community is what is most important. Therefore, a communion ecclesiology from below needs to take note of this fact. It must be constructed in light of this fact. Miguel Díaz forcefully affirms this in his essay "Outside the Survival of Community There Is No Salvation: A U.S. Hispanic Catholic Contribution to Soteriology."[32] The grace of God cannot be separated from the community of God's people. It is there where God's grace is planted, grows, and spreads. This is why the cultural and religious dynamics of fiestas within the Latino communities are crucial to the reimagining of our identity as a hopeful communion of faith. Fiestas should be understood and re-examined for our affirmation and practice of Eucharistic *koinōnia*.

Why are fiestas the focus point for our discussion? Fiestas are the fertile ground where Latino identity springs forth. They express who we are as we celebrate life together. Here I can only briefly summarize some of the most crucial dynamics within a fiesta that

31. I already discussed this issue in more detail in chapter 1 of this book. Cf. in particular Elizondo, "Mestizaje as a Locus of Theological Reflection," 162–63.

32. Miguel Díaz, "Outside the Survival of Community There Is No Salvation: A U.S. Hispanic Catholic Contribution to Soteriology," in Espín, ed., *Building Bridges, Doing Justice*, 91–93. Díaz offers a clever new interpretation of the phrase coined by Cyprian of Carthage, bishop in North Africa, during the third century: "extra Ecclesiam nulla salus" (there is no salvation outside the church). Cyprian affirmed that Jesus established the one church and the one church serves as that institution where the grace of God is communicated to the world. Díaz affirms the presence of the communion of the people of God where Christ dwells as the head and foundation of the church. It is the people living in Christ's community where the church lives and redemption is found.

forge our identity in living together. Fiestas are not for Latinos mere "parties," where moments are enjoyed to forget the present predicament or situation. Fiestas are not a series of wanton joys. Our fiestas are occasions where we celebrate life. We celebrate events that mark the gift of life from God among us. We celebrate in essence how we are bound together as a community and a people. This may be discerned in our celebrations of events in Jesus's life, births, baptisms, weddings, saints' days, *quinceañeras*, funerals, and many other events. Our fiestas provide a sacred space. The participation in Latino fiestas notably blurs the distinction or dualism between civil and religious celebrations.[33] Fiestas are occasions for thanksgiving for having received life. Therefore, they express, as Roberto Goizueta suggests, "a profound sense of the human in relationship to the Sacred."[34]

During our fiestas we are able to welcome the gifts of each member of the community for the sake of our living together within the community at that time and place. Goizueta identifies the gifts received and shared. There is an intrinsic connection "between the gift and its Giver."[35] This gift of life is concrete for it is grounded in the love of the Creator toward us and in our active response to that love. This response is evident in our acts of celebration. This is because during these acts of celebration, our fiestas, the last is lifted up to become the first or very valuable member of our community. This is evident, for example, in the *quinceañera* (the celebration of the fifteenth birthday of a young Latina). It is a celebration and thanks-

---

33. Roberto S. Goizueta, "Fiesta: Life in the Subjunctive," in Espín and Díaz, eds., *From the Heart of Our People*, 84–99. Goizueta provides a constructive apologetics to answer the concepts of self and identity in modernity and postmodernity. My efforts are directed to the present state of affairs in church life in the United States, focusing on factors that hinder a Eucharistic *koinōnia*. See also Isasi-Díaz, *La Lucha Continues*, where she reflects on and applies this communion from a "Mujerista Christological Understanding" (240–66).

34. Goizueta, "Fiesta," 85.

35. Goizueta, "Fiesta," 91.

giving for God's gift of her life. She is acknowledged as an integral member of that community. She is also asked to accept those duties of life, given by God, to build the family and the community of faith.[36]

In terms of the celebration of fiestas in Latino communities there are definite major elements from a Catholic popular religiosity.[37] A key to these celebrations is the centrality of the cross as a concrete manifestation of the irreducible gift of life from God to us.[38] These celebrations are usually marked, therefore, by an active response and resolve to love our neighbor concretely in all aspects of life. In this context, therefore, the poor are valued, for God pours out his gifts on the total community in order for those gifts to be celebrated.

Fiestas also provide further opportunities for our *convivir*, for they become an opportune time to welcome strangers and guests to participate as integral valuable members of our community as we celebrate life together. The poor are not accepted because of some magnanimous effort from the rich but because they are in that celebration integral members of the community. The poor, the less educated, children, and women are also able to work and play as valuable members of the community. In essence, the status quo is challenged because the distinction of classes is blurred or set aside during the celebration. There is a real affirmation of the outcast as a gift from God. Fiestas usually become in these dynamics a sacred space for new real possibilities within the community. There is, as Goizueta observes, "an attitude of trust in the ultimate goodness of

36. See Angela Erevia, *Quinceañera* (San Antonio, TX: Mexican American Center, 1980), 15-25. Goizueta comments on this work and from other personal observations concerning the value of this festive observation.

37. See the first chapter in this book. This is clearly expressed in the celebration of patron saints.

38. This is very much present also in the celebration of the *quinceañera* (see note 36 above). This is articulated especially in most celebrations of the *quinceañera* by an invocation to the Trinity and by affirming the binding of the community through their shared baptism in Christ's death and resurrection.

life."[39] We may describe this as a latent sense of an "eschatological hope." This is why Goizueta describes fiestas as "life in the subjunctive." There is a definite celebration of the present where work and play come together as a real present possibility for acceptance and change. The community affected in this action is projected into the future in hope of overcoming the present alienations that will inevitably come into play again when the fiesta ends because of our human condition. But this celebration of life cannot end or stop for people of the faith who live an ongoing celebration of the sacramental life. This celebration of life becomes ever more present for those who share the real presence of the crucified and risen Christ within the *koinōnia* of the body of Christ. We need to reimagine this *koinōnia* in light of the apocalyptic hope called for in 1 Corinthians.

Living Our *Koinōnia* in Apocalyptic Hope

There is a wall today in North America that is becoming higher and higher, preventing Latino families and communities from joining in a common celebration of life with other members of the body of Christ. Many social and ecclesial conditions exist that threaten the very identity of Latino families and communities in this state of affairs. I have already outlined some of these problems in my previous chapters in this volume. The issues of immigration, hate crimes, lack of access to gainful employment, and poor education are among these social issues. There are many civic and political leaders who claim to be Christians who view with suspicion the presence of Latino families in the United States. This is especially demonstrated in the invisible or visible fences created within their communities of faith. This is why many Latinos view with suspicion and fear what is going on in our churches. Miguel Díaz poignantly observes how, "on the religious side, Latino/a families often find

39. Goizueta, "Fiesta," 96.

themselves alienated in churches and in sacramental 'celebrations.'"[40] How does this take place and how can we apply for this time and place Paul's reflections in 1 Corinthians?

The celebration of the Eucharist no longer takes place in homes. There are no *agapē* meals beforehand where the rich and people of high status do what they want and in essence "humiliate those who have nothing" (1 Cor. 11:22). However, a great majority of our North American churches are not even aware that their liturgy and practice and the way they conduct themselves prevent the stranger and the immigrant from participating and becoming integral members of their communities. During Pope Francis's visit to the United States I heard many of my Latino Catholic friends talk about how the liturgy and worship in most of those worship events practically ignored the participation and talents of US Latino Catholics. Today the spirit of xenophobia is growing day by day in our North American communities. North American Christians, of every stripe and persuasion, speak out against undocumented Latinos in printed form or on social media, showing their suspicion and resentment against them, and even calling them criminals. This resentment has also been directed toward Latinos who have lived in the United States for more than one generation, preventing them from becoming full members of the body of Christ. These new "Corinthian" Christians in essence are eating first their *agapē* meal and also preventing marginal faithful Christians from coming and joining their fellowship. The pilgrims living in the borderlands, therefore, view with suspicion the actions of love and fellowship coming from those centers of worship.

It is becoming harder and harder, therefore, to welcome Latinos in our churches, as many Latino pastors and missionaries bear testimony, because Latinos are suspicious of our actions toward them. This creates walls, obstacles that prevent the most vulnerable from coming to the table to share in the Eucharist. This practice and

40. Díaz, "Outside the Survival of Community," 100.

attitude is in essence not any different from what was practiced in Corinth during New Testament times. Paul condemns this practice. In fact, this practice of excluding the faithful from coming to the table is what rejects the real presence of the body and blood for us.[41] This is in fact what Paul condemns as "eating the bread and drinking the blood in an unworthy manner" (1 Cor. 11:27). The proper eating and drinking is not a mere affirmation of a formula that describes how the body and blood of Christ are present. The present and final goal is to be bound in this *koinōnia* of faith that acts out Christ's incarnational presence in a new festive hope. This is what Paul affirms: "This cup is the new covenant in my blood. Do this [*hagan esto*], as often as you drink [*beban*] it, in remembrance of me. For as often as you eat [*coman*] this bread and drink [*beban*] the cup, you proclaim [*proclaman*] the Lord's death until he comes" (1 Cor. 11:25a–26). Again, I take note of this imperative given to the community of faith in hopeful expectation.

New Testament research for the past two generations has properly emphasized that in the whole New Testament the Lord's Supper is the anticipation on earth of the messianic banquet. The texts in Mark 14:25 and 1 Corinthians 11:26 need to be read in light of this eschatological and festive hope for the parousia. This is very much found in 1 Corinthians 16:22: *Marana tha* (Come, O Lord). But it is more than a festive celebration grounded in an eschatological hope. It is also more than a remembrance within our consciousness

41. The confessional Lutheran theologian Edmund Schlink in his classic work *Theology of the Lutheran Confessions*, trans. Paul F. Koehneke and Herbert J. A. Bouman (Philadelphia: Fortress, 1961), underscores the very nature of the church in this active incarnational *koinōnia*. The very nature and gift of the hearing of the gospel and participation in the sacraments is that "the brothers are in a fellowship—and their fellowship is a sharing of each other's grace and burden." The very essence of being the church is the "mutual giving of oneself to the other and working for the other in love has its basis in the common hearing of the Gospel through which the Holy Spirit gives love together with faith, and this faith unites the believers into one body" (204). Cf. Cheryl M. Peterson, "Lutheran Principles for Ecclesiology," in García and Wood, eds., *Critical Issues in Ecclesiology*, 156–59.

of Christ's death and resurrection. It is a celebration of Christ's real presence. Because we celebrate Christ's real presence, these celebrations in effect include a present fulfillment of our future and complete expectations.[42]

This eschatological dimension has not been lifted up enough in our proclamation and action because many Christians fear how it is presented in the New Testament and by the Reformation within an apocalyptic drama. In this drama there is a struggle between good and evil, between God's forces and the demonic powers. Luther lived this vision and many times demonized people and institutions in light of his understanding of the apocalyptic drama.[43] In effect Luther sometimes acted as an "end-time prophet" and so drove people away from the fellowship of the kingdom by demonizing them. There is no doubt that he was definitely powerfully influenced by the popular apocalyptic literature of the later Middle Ages. There is for Luther, however, a definite engagement of the new kingdom of God in history. He sometimes interpreted this *novum regnum* in light of the prophecies of Ezekiel and Daniel.[44] However, his attempt to relate eschatology to the course of history was confusing. This is much the case in his second preface to the book of Revelation (1545). Luther also accented the final abrupt consummation of God's kingdom.[45]

---

42. See Herman Sasse, *We Confess the Sacraments*, trans. Norman Nagel (St. Louis: Concordia, 1985), 92–93. Ernst Käsemann poignantly underscored this point in his programmatic essay "Die Anfängechristlicher Theologie" when he affirmed that "the apocalyptic was the mother of all Christian theology." See Westhelle, *The Scandalous God*, 156.

43. Jane E. Strohl, "Luther's Eschatology," in *The Oxford Handbook of Martin Luther's Theology*, ed. Robert Kolb, Irene Dingel, and L'Ubomír Batka (Oxford: Oxford University Press, 2014), 355–56; Hinlicky, *Luther and the Beloved Community*, 383–84

44. T. F. Torrance, "The Eschatological Faith: Martin Luther," in *Luther: Theologian for Catholics and Protestants*, ed. George Hule (Edinburgh: T&T Clark, 1985), 154. Cf. *WA* 11/1:392.

45. Torrance, "The Eschatological Faith," 154. Torrance attributes this to the influence of scholastic philosophy and the theological conception of eternity as "totum simul, alles auf einmal" (all at one place or same time and place).

Paul's eschatological teaching of God's imminent new creation, however, provided for Luther a distinctive apocalyptic hope. The Apocalypse also spelled out for Luther a promise of inclusion of the despised in God's coming reign by the grace of Christ. This point of departure permitted Luther to reject the traditional conflicting dualisms proclaimed at the time between flesh and spirit, creation and redemption. Heiko Oberman argues that in general this is a correct way to read Luther's legacy for today.[46] This legacy needs to be understood and reimagined for our times. This is crucial for our appropriation of *koinōnia* from the margins.

Carl Braaten clarifies how our hopeful expectation, our eschatological hope, needs to be understood in terms of the recovery of an apocalyptic imagination. He perceptively draws from the work of John Collins to apply an apocalyptic imagination for our times.[47] Collins writes:

> The apocalyptic revolution is a revolution in the imagination. It entails a challenge to view the world in a way that is radically different from the common perception. The revolutionary potential of such imagination should not be underestimated, as it can foster dissatisfaction with the present and generate visions of what might be. The legacy of the apocalypses includes a powerful rhetoric for denouncing the deficiencies of this world. It also includes the conviction that the world as now constituted is not the end. Most of all, it entails an appreciation of the great resource that lies in the human imagination to construct a symbolic world where the integrity of values can be maintained in

46. As discussed in Hinlicky, *Luther and the Beloved Community*, 382. See also along these lines Claus Schwambach, *Rechtfertigungsgeschehen und Befreiungs prozess: Die Eschatologien von Martin Luther und Leonardo Boff im kritischen Gespräch* (Göttingen: Vandenhoeck & Ruprecht, 2004), 100–104.

47. Braaten, *That All May Believe*, 123.

the face of social and political powerlessness and even of the threat of death.[48]

The reality is that we cannot read the eschatology of the New Testament apart from an apocalyptic framework. This apocalyptic hermeneutical key has been cast aside and neglected today in light of modern cosmologies. Braaten, following Collins, affirms the apocalyptic imagination as crucial to denouncing the present deficiencies in our world and keeping a firm resolve that the present evil we face is not the end. There is hope for change now in view of this future.

This language is very much alive in many Latino churches, in particular, the growing Pentecostal communities in the Americas. I have visited several Lutheran congregations in Latin America and the Caribbean that have been influenced by this resolve and apocalyptic language. In their liturgical services there comes a time when pastors and the priesthood of all believers renounce by the power of the Spirit those evil powers present that are hindering the community. They do so through a poetic cadence and resolve.[49] They call out through these living litanies for present change and a final

48. As quoted in Braaten, *That All May Believe*, 123–24. Cf. John J. Collins, *The Apocalyptic Imagination: An Introduction to Jewish Apocalyptic Literature*, 2nd ed. (Grand Rapids: Eerdmans, 1998), 283.

49. We may find this living litany of apocalyptic faith in the song "La Vida es un Carnaval," written by the late Cuban recording artist Celia Cruz, Sergio George, and Victor Daniel. This song became Cruz's living hope toward the end of her life. The song was sung as a final tribute to her during her funeral at Saint Patrick's Cathedral in New York. The role of carnival as a subversive fiesta has been discussed and analyzed by Victor Turner. Goizueta appropriates this study to analyze the role of fiesta among Latinos. See Goizueta, "Fiesta," 93–94. However, Cruz's song goes further. It is a litany in the celebration of life. She points out the possibility of ending inequalities and ills in life. It is a hopeful expectation offered in a rhythmic cadence where the singer calls out to end and remove those ills and evils, receiving an immediate response from the other musicians and audience: "*fuera*" (leave us!—this is what is implied by the colloquial sound). In a sense Cruz approximates the apocalyptic imagination addressed in this section.

end to those ills and evils that shatter their identity and meaning as a community of faith.[50] These expectations conform to the New Testament apocalyptic vision and the reimagining of *koinōnia* from the margins. But these litanies, as well as our evangelical catholic, Catholic, and Protestant proclamation of the gospel, tend to turn into finding demons or scapegoats for our maladies. Our dissatisfaction with the present evils and injustices must be driven by an apocalyptic imagination that calls for change. The present is not the end. But this driven apocalyptic hope must be lived in a cruciform existence in order not to specially demonize those at the margins who call for just change within their borders.

The present place where the people of God are gathered is able to offer under the cross a different possibility for people. This can be done only when the present powers of evil and sin are unmasked. The seemingly good that is supposed to unite the community of faith in fact hinders it, and must be called out for what it is. In the words of Luther under the cross the "good" must be called "bad." Those who have been kept away from the community of faith because they truly live and proclaim God's newness of life driven by their apocalyptic hope must be called "good" instead of "bad."[51] In other words, it is possible that those strangers, foreigners, who seem to be the scum of the earth, might be the bearers of the apocalyp-

50. In eastern Africa the Lutheran denominations are growing at a rapid rate and are more numerous than the present North American Lutheran denominations. I believe that part of their success is how they proclaim and act their faith life through similar living litanies of faith.

51. Vitor Westhelle offers a similar connection of Luther's theology of the cross to appropriate the New Testament apocalyptic eschatological vision for our times. See *The Scandalous God*, 156–58. He appropriates and enhances in a sense the state of "liminality" present in the celebration among Latino communities. Cf. Goizueta's discussion on liminality in "Fiesta," 92–93. The cross disrupts, turns upside down, collective efforts to exclude the margins, creating new spaces of possibilities for the now present apocalyptic hope. An important work that relates for today and especially in Latin America the connection of Luther's theology of the cross to eschatology is Schwambach, *Rechtfertigungsgeschehen und Befreiungsprozess*, 48–50.

tic-driven hope that our faith community needs to hear in order to acknowledge the binding presence of our coming Lord. But this good word comes under the cross and in the cruciform way of life that we need to hear and welcome in our midst. It is in this way of life that we live our unity under the Spirit of God.

The apocalyptic vision and language in the New Testament binds the Christian community in the power of the Spirit to "be strong in the Lord and in the strength of his power . . . [to] struggle [not only] against enemies of blood and flesh, but [also] against the rulers, against the authorities, against the cosmic powers of this present darkness" (Eph. 6:10–12). Again, the force of the text is that the whole community of faith is asked to "be strong" (*fortaleceos* = imperative second-person plural, in Greek and Spanish) and "take up" (*tomad* = imperative second-person plural) "the whole armor of God." The whole Christian community is called together to struggle and reject those things that prevent the community of faith from being God's constructive and caring community of faith. Paul also urges this practice in the reality of the Eucharist (1 Cor. 11:27–33). In essence, Paul is asking the community to remove those elements and situations from their communal life that reject the caring, impacting presence of the incarnate Christ. It is in this resolve that the church engages in festive hope. It is not a naïve or utopian hope, for this festive hope calls for God's final (apocalyptic) outcome. Paul declares: "For as often as you [the gathered community of faith] eat this bread and drink the cup, you proclaim the Lord's death until he comes" (1 Cor. 11:26). In other words, our communities of faith are able to continue their festive hope, by celebrating the real present possibilities that exist to eliminate our alienations, albeit tentative due to our human condition, in light of our cruciform existence that calls out always in living hope: Maranatha! There is hope at this time and place for change in this communion, life together, of the justified.

CHAPTER 8

Koinōnia and Diversity

....

Postcolonial Poetics of the Possible

Why is there so much public and private conversation in the United States, including among Christians, about race and ethnicity? Perhaps it is precisely because of the United States' foundational claims concerning itself as a model of ethnic pluralism. Depending on the criteria being used and who is doing the reporting, there are more different kinds of people here than anywhere else in the world.[1] They enjoy unparalleled opportunities for social mobility, the narrative goes, as they live, love, work, play, and pray in proximity and peace with one another.

Ironically, it is this very diversity—magnified by the global, public prominence of the United States and impelled by the exceptional promise of *e pluribus unum*—that serves to make more obvious in the United States the pockets of resistance breaking faith with our national experiment. This is especially glaring among those holding to false religions of racism. The higher the bar is set, the more blatant is the missing of the mark. The louder the trumpet of

1. Human diversity is a fluid and dynamic concept—without a single or simple definition. It is related to how humans understand, interpret, accept, and respect differences and alterity; these include, but are not limited to, ethnicity, race, gender, sexual orientation, socioeconomic status, age, physical ability, political beliefs, religious beliefs, and ideology.

freedom and opportunity sounds, the more the discordant notes of exclusion or oppression jangle.

Further, recalcitrant expressions of ecclesial, ethnic mono-culturalism, in the shadows of the gospel's inclusive luminosity, both challenge and embarrass the church on earth as it considers its radical commitment to a new, non-race-based way of being in community, namely, *koinōnia*. This faith-formed way of doing life together, Dietrich Bonhoeffer taught us, is not based on external similarities to one another, or immediacy of closeness, or any other virtuous ingredient in the community itself—including its diver-sity—but is based in Jesus Christ alone. "We belong to one another only through and in Jesus Christ"[2] and "there is never . . . an 'imme-diate' relationship of one to another."[3] Hence, Bonhoeffer informs our present topic, helping us see that those lovers of diversity in itself preempt genuine communal diversity, while those who love Christ first possess the single constitutive factor needed to sustain diverse communities. (More discussion can be found later in this chapter under the subheading "Paying Attention to the Excessive Love of Diversity.")

In his review of Terry Eagleton's *Culture and the Death of God*, the former chief rabbi of the Commonwealth of Nations Jonathan Sacks, writing in the *Jewish Review of Books*, muses: "Too little has been done within the faith traditions themselves to make space for the kind of diversity with which we will have to live if humankind is to have a future."[4] These words, at a minimum, form an echo of Martin Luther King Jr.'s prophetic axiom, "If we cannot learn to live together as sisters and brothers we will surely perish apart as fools." Both Sacks and King point toward an epistemological and ontological challenge: deliberation about diversity should be rooted in material from within one's own tradition; interpreters keen for

2. Bonhoeffer, *Life Together*, 31.
3. Bonhoeffer, *Life Together*, 41.
4. Jonathan Sacks, "Nostalgia for the Numinous" (a review of Terry Eagleton's *Culture and the Death of God*), *Jewish Review of Books* 18 (Summer 2014).

a convivial future should be redemptive re-translators of their own theological heritage spoken anew in application to today's pluralistic contexts. Too much theological conversation about diversity in contemporary society fails because it comes with baggage derived from arenas of life not related to theology (culture, politics, etc.). Lutheran intellectuals, lagging in their development of theological categories to unpack that baggage, should begin, therefore, *within* their tradition, echoing the critically modernist Søren Kierkegaard, who spoke of the healing found within the wound.

The five-hundredth anniversary of the beginning of the Reformation represents a point in time, in 2017, in which the average global Lutheran looks more like an East African than like a German or white North American. Lutherans in the United States find themselves in a conundrum if not crisis: they are located ecclesiastically in a tradition committed foremost to being confessional and evangelical catholic—nothing in their identity is defined by, or is exclusionary of, any race or ethnicity. Further, they are located demographically in a nation experiencing increasing diversity—the United States was 85 percent white in 1960 and will be 43 percent white in 2060.[5] Yet, amid these realities, US Lutherans are the most white and English-speaking religious group in the nation.[6] My argument here is that this moment offers possibility as we engage the global church to be a resource, nudging us toward a reimagined consideration of what constitutes the church, what the sine qua non of the *communio sanctorum* is. I believe the Holy Spirit will use our engagement with these others to prompt us toward a deeper

5. http://mic.com/articles/87819/what-will-america-look-like-in-2060-9-bold-predictions-about-our-future.

6. This statistic is verified by multiple research entities over decades. This first surfaced in formal research in Exhibit 13 of the American Religious Identification Survey of 2001. It was reconfirmed in 2015 with the LCMS edging out the ELCA by a fraction (http://commons.trincoll.edu/aris/surveys/aris-2001/; http://www.pewresearch.org/fact-tank/2015/07/27/the-most-and-least-racially-diverse-u-s-religious-groups/).

understanding and practice of biblical and confessional notions of ecclesial diversity.

What follows are six theologically infused, practical considerations to which we can pay attention.

Paying Attention to the Image of God

From the Lutheran-Christian perspective, valuing others is squarely predicated on the understanding of the image of God.[7] Germane, again, is Dietrich Bonhoeffer; he offers a note in his commentary on Genesis, proposing a framework for the image of God, beyond *analogia entis*, or the analogy of being—that the image of God is realized ontologically, fixed in humans like a miniature mirror of the divine. It should not be overlooked that many of Bonhoeffer's first readers resided in Nazi Germany, a nation in which human dignity was under siege. To them he delivered the prophetic reminder that the image of God also implies the *analogia relationis*, or the analogy of relationality—that God's image is realized fluidly in human community as we relate to one another with dignity and reflect the divine being, three persons in one God.[8]

All people, especially minorities, are conscious of situations in which they are welcomed or endangered, disrespected or valued. All people gravitate naturally toward communities in which their

7. The fullness of the *imago Dei* "in, with, and under" every human person carries the corresponding dynamic of every individual's right to be regarded with dignity within every cultural context. Hackmann defines the human person within an Augustinian framework as a "being imaging the essence of God, of unconditional worth, characterized by a complex of internal and external relationships which are integrated into a unity of being, relation, and activity." E. Edward Hackmann, "Augustine and the Concept of Person," *Lutheran Theological Review* 3, no. 2 (Spring–Summer 1991): 25.

8. Dietrich Bonhoeffer, *Creation and Fall: A Theological Exposition of Genesis 1–3*, ed. John W. de Gruchy, trans. Douglas Stephen Bax, Dietrich Bonhoeffer Works 3 (Minneapolis: Fortress, 1997), 64–65.

contributions are recognized and respected. Luther's catechetical ethics is ingenious not only in proscribing sin, the avoidance of evil, but also in prescribing its opposite, the pursuit of good. Racism, then, not only includes sins of commission—diminishing the value, values, and contributions of a group—but also can involve sins of omission—exaggerating or overstating the value, values, and contributions of one group while willfully excluding or ignoring those of others. In a pluralistic society, this ethical consideration should be taken seriously, paid attention to, among those who bear the image of God and recognize it in others, especially "outsiders."

Paying Attention to Affinities

While it may be perfectly natural, from an anthropological perspective, for humans to react to the other with responses ranging from mild suspicion to paranoid cynicism, this behavior tends to confirm original sin, namely, that an individual's or a group's fundamental reference becomes incurved (*incurvatio in seipsum*), turned to itself, rather than oriented toward the neighbor as an extension of its orientation outward toward Christ. Those others who have been made new creatures in Christ are no longer evaluated by outward criteria (2 Cor. 5:16).

As we saw in Chapter 6, in the church's life together, we must exercise constant vigilance to be sure that no one particular cultural expression becomes a primary unifier, filtering out of the fellowship those who are different, rather than *life together* unifying the church in Christ, with a common confession of faith, as agents of Christ through radical lives of *witness* and *service*. Even human goods such as "great learning, wisdom, power, prestige, family and honor"[9] can become false gods if they are pursued apart from God, apart from

---

9. Martin Luther, *Large Catechism* (*BC*, 387).

the deliverance of Jesus Christ, apart from the Holy Spirit's enlightenment. Not only are these priorities unable to sustain and nurture
the sort of life God intends us to live, but they can become invisible fences that exclude those lacking these virtues, thus preventing
koinōnia. Without the tempering effect of a spirituality of stewardship, proud egos will create a God from any good.

Lutherans fall short when the impression is given that Lutheran
identity is tantamount to Nordic and Germanic cultural values,
which, though they can be in themselves *goods*, cannot save humans
or the church. By this is inferred musical forms, literacy, artistic
style, punctiliousness, even humor (Garrison Keillor-esque refer-
ences, Lena and Ole!).Without the incursion of outsiders, strangers,
and new neighbors, redemptive truth often is not perceived but
becomes diluted by its enmeshment with cultural values.

Paying Attention to the Excessive Love of Diversity

Yet, caution must be taken by those seeking intentionally to create inclusion, those overly valuing diversity. The risk for lovers
of diversity is their tendency to define the "other" according to
a category, as an essential type, in such a way that forecloses the
possibility of knowing authentically the others because they are
now encapsulated within an ontological and definitional framework that erects finite barriers preventing them from being fully
and truly known. Such an approach to diversity represents an ontological escapism, a misrepresentation and misrecognition due
to an a priori abstract ideal that ignores the concrete, real human
person standing right before us and the hegemonic structures that
incarcerate individuals in reductionist containers of anonymity.
It is irrational to highlight the ultimate specialness of any general
group's cultural ethnicity if that highlighting is over against the
one race to which we all belong, called human. This insidiously
racialized Gnosticism manifests itself in incommensurable claims

like "it's a black thing, you wouldn't understand," or "mirror, mirror on the wall, who's the most Latino of us all?" European supremacist narratives likewise perpetuate exclusiveness made more pernicious because they transgress the Creator's non-prejudicial redemption of a common humanity.

Bonhoeffer counsels in *Life Together* against the anticipatory, tribalist stereotyping of the other: "I can never know in advance how God's image should appear in others. . . . Rather this diversity is a reason for rejoicing in one another and serving one another."[10] Human diversity, then, is not static, a set of goals, categories to be predicated, boxes to be checked, containers to be filled, but diversity for Christians bears a reflective image of the divinity, the Trinitarian God, providing a fluid template of loving service as it values in love the lives of others, and gives full-throated, full-hearted, fully terrestrial, interdependent praise to the God of love who loves the diverse creation.

Paying Attention to Definitions of Diversity

An enduring definition of diversity, from a Christian perspective, is that which values others inherently as fellow humans worthy of respect despite and even within the full range of our differences, but not because of differences. The problem with valuing others in an unqualified manner because or due to the fact that they are different is the limit of recourse to disassociate that respect from those types of diversity and difference considered objectionable—for example, when in the name of diversity someone violates intentionally other humans, transgresses Christian ethics, or destroys creation. While we should continue to value those others as human persons, it constitutes, however, an absurd violation of conscience to value them because of their diversity. That would be tantamount to valuing a

10. Bonhoeffer, *Life Together*, 95.

difference determined to be destructive.[11] It is not merely difference qua difference that is valued, it is people as people and people despite difference.

Paying Attention to Networks

Despite its ethnic enclaves, the Lutheran Church describes itself, as a matter of confession, as a body not defined by national boundaries[12] or racial lines; it is not an association "like other civic organizations"[13] but is composed of those who are sanctified by the Spirit, from all times and places, participating in God's holy things.[14] The church is a unique society of the redeemed, joined together because they are first and foremost united with Jesus Christ by baptism.

The Ten Commandments, correlated to the structures of creation, guide the community of faith in its reflection on the manner in which it organizes itself. The church, like the world, is God's,

---

11. Though simple, I find this acrostic not simplistic, but a useful teaching tool for diversity:

D ifferent
I ndividuals
V aluing
E ach other
R egardless of
S kin
I dentity
T alent or
Y ears

12. Since the church "consists of people scattered throughout the entire world who agree on the gospel and have the same Christ, the same Holy Spirit, and the same sacraments," why are so many Protestant denominations, including Lutherans in the United States, organized according to the geopolitical boundaries of contemporary nation-states? See *AP* VII–VIII, in *BC*, 175.

13. *AP* VII, in *BC*, 174.

14. See note 13 regarding "the communion of the saints" in *The Three Ecumenical Creeds* (*BC*, 22).

grounded by God in Christ who is the Creator and Sustainer of all persons, all relationships, all systems—there are no unsupervised processes in the universe, including the manner in which humans associate. Luther explains that the ninth and tenth commandments are not intended for the common folk, but for the elite, the decision-makers,[15] those who appear virtuous, yet "practice bribery through friendly connections."[16] Since socioeconomic poverty is often defined as a lack of access to education, opportunity, technology, resources, and information, being locked out of networks of success by such "friendly connections" and insider referrals can have implications, for example, contributing to structural racism.

Paying Attention to the Trajectory of the Narrative

Narratives of negativity about the direction of the quality of life and freedoms enjoyed in the United States may say more about one's personal estimation of power and privilege and its loss than they do about the actual facts of this nation's historical trajectory. These narratives, the stories we tell ourselves and others to make sense of reality, should be always tested against the persistent hope of the gospel, the promises of God's providential presence in time, and the victory of the resurrection that pervades all eternity.

More practically, for the vast majority of visible minorities and recent immigrants, life now is better than ever and life here in the United States is better than anywhere else in the world. Personally, "as for me and my house," we would much rather be alive now than at any point in the history we have both studied and experienced firsthand. Further, having traveled much of the world, I would

15. "This last commandment, therefore, is not addressed to those whom the world considers wicked rogues, but precisely to the most upright—to people who wish to be commended as honest and virtuous because they have not offended against the preceding commandments." *Large Catechism* (*BC*, 426).

16. *Large Catechism* (*BC*, 427).

rather reside here in the United States than in any other country in the world that I have experienced. Consequently, the narratives of most immigrants and minorities within the United States, despite the shortcomings, economic struggles, and criminal justice crises, are positive, ones of possibility and improvement.

When the narratives of US Lutherans focus primarily on signs of decline, this creates a degree of misalignment with minorities and immigrants difficult to overcome. When the Lutheran worldview differs so drastically in matters related to this nation's trajectory regarding its economic, sociological, cultural, and political direction, this makes it difficult to establish the common ground needed for evangelistic witness, outreach, and hospitable fellowship to develop. Gospel opportunities are lost because of worldview incongruity.

A Poetics of the Possible

Koinōnia, the sense of being a community of diverse persons, is formed, impelled, and brought to completion in the person and work of Jesus Christ. Such diversity is a gift that transcends human categories. This evangelical catholic approach to diversity, while not unintentional, is not about thin representationalism (quotas or cultural phenomena) but about thick respect for all the baptized, a theologically determined inclusion, motivated by a deep commitment to Scripture, confessions, the gospel, and church history and grounded in an expansive, eschatological, global approach to ecclesial identity.

What follows are two attempts to convey a narrated experience that proposes a poetics of the possible as a schema for paying attention to, interpreting, and advocating for diversity.

Narrative 1: Paying Attention to Diversity

It was the heart of a hot August. I should have been fatigued as I rolled my luggage bags from the rental car lot to the Delta Airlines terminal, but the buoyant bounce in my stride spoke for itself. I was impervious to the heavy Manitoba heat. I had just lectured at an event and it had gone refreshingly well.

A man with a welcoming Winnipeg smile partly hidden beneath his prairie whiskers pointed me and other Minneapolis-bound travelers toward a sign with an arrow reading, "United States Immigration." In Canada? I mused mind-roamingly to myself. I hadn't seen anything like this anywhere in the world; there was certainly no US immigration desk in the Netaji Subhas Chandra Bose International Airport—a diversion I mention only to draw attention to how much I like this serious name, after a postcolonial Indian hero, as contrasted with the sillier, almost incredible name of Kolkata's airport during the colonialist era, Dum Dum Airport.

But a US immigration desk in Canada? I guess Canada—quite unlike the United States' southern neighbor, Mexico—occupies some special space as our friendly neighbors, the nation with the nickname "Great White North"—another diversion, this one to draw attention to how much I don't like that double-edged sobriquet for Canada.

A US immigration desk in Canada is a rather useful metaphor—people can be theoretically permitted back into the United States, they can even hear those words, "Welcome home," while, spatially, they haven't even boarded the plane to leave Canada yet. This is a geographic analogy for living eschatologically, in a state of time and eternity, simultaneously, a sequential suspension of the "now" and the "not yet," at the same time, having fully arrived while still on the journey, having fully realized that humans are one people, but with plenty of diversity work left to do with 646 nautical miles to go, or as most of the world, including Canada, might commonly measure that distance, 1,039 nautical kilometers.

As I leaned forward in the line, trying hard to appear casual as a disguise for my eavesdropping, I heard the tall US immigration agent speaking in German to a traveler. Waiting, I tried to recall my limited German vocabulary because it never hurts to relate in a friendly way to a man in a uniform who could ruin your day.

By now I was daydreaming; imagine me, a fake German-speaking, Jamaica-born, US citizen being denied entry to my own country while yet in the country where I was raised, where my parents even now currently live, in Canada.

I imagined hearing the judgment: "You are not permitted to leave your former home to go back to your current home, so now go to your parents' home." As my brain was about to pop at the existential possibilities, my turn came, and with no one behind me I strode, fully prepared, with elation, toward the desk: "Güten Tag, Herr . . ."—eyes down to his name-tag, "Herr Hong?" "Oh," I continued, in English, "I know that name, Hong, in fact, Howard and Edna Hong—translators of one of my favorite philosophers, Søren Kierkegaard."

"You know the name Hong, do you?" he probed, peering down his nose through his drugstore reading glasses, eyes narrowing in a winced pause, then quizzically widening. I could see him swallowing hard. A pause. Then he looked around, and in a non-official, non-immigration-agent tone, said something more unimaginable than the absurd scenario I was painting in my mind while standing in line: "Those would be my dear, deceased parents. How in the world do you know them?"

"Well, I don't know them," I managed to stutter in some shocked staccato tone, "but I've cited them in enough bibliographies to never forget them. Their work saved Kierkegaard for the English-speaking world."

Glancing back over my shoulder, I saw no one behind me in the queue so I knew I had time to "talk Kierkegaard" with one of the few everyday human beings who appreciated this Danish philosopher and theologian more than me. So, I told him about a paper I once wrote in a graduate-level course in which I got an A, a course on Kierkegaard taught by Antje Jackelén (who was, by the way, in 2013 elected as the first woman to be Archbishop of Sweden). I was previously her teaching assistant—a diversion I added simply for the purposes of name-dropping. In this paper I compared Kierkegaard's work with postcolonialism—and Herr Hong was at least appearing to be interested.

"And what did you write?"

"Well, I'm glad you asked." I obliged him and continued. "Both existentialism and postcolonialism are concerned with dilemmas of existence like identity and personal meaning, the individual's posture vis-à-vis eternal things, but at times," I continued, accelerating to an almost lecture-like cadence, "existentialism presents itself a bit too fancifully for the postcolonialist, not taking seriously legacies of suffering, the history of oppression, paying too much attention to the individual, her or his personal dread, prone to miss the place of community and alterity."

"You've got a point there?" replied Hong graciously, in what sounded more like a question. So I kept talking. "Derek Walcott, the world's greatest poet, is right, existentialism can degrade itself into a sort of 'myth of the noble savage gone baroque.'"[17]

---

17. The quotation of Derek Walcott ensues from a discussion of history, its attendant visions of progress, and the myths associated with the postcolonial conjunction of the Old and New Worlds. Ironically, Walcott here employs the idea of absurdity existentially even in debunking any notion of postcolonial existentialism: "The blasphemous images fade, because these hieroglyphs of progress are basically comic. And if the idea of the New and the Old becomes increasingly absurd, what must happen to our sense of time, what else can happen to history itself, but that it, too, is becoming absurd? This is not existentialism. Adamic, elemental man cannot be existential. His first impulse is not self-indulgence but awe, and existentialism is simply the myth of the noble savage gone baroque. Existential philosophies of freedom are born in cities. Existentialism is as much nostalgia as in Rousseau's sophisticated primitivism, as sick as recurrence in French thought as the Ilse of Cythera, whether it is the tubercular, fevered imagery of Watteau or the same fever turned delirious in Rimbaud and Baudelaire" (Walcott, *What the Twilight Says*, 41–42).

At that point, someone who looked like a supervisor began to do his own eavesdropping and Mr. Hong's next words to me were, "May I see your passport, sir?" Our feast had ended. But not without me inviting him to Valparaiso University to talk with my students about his parents.

After I got home, I dug out some old Kierkegaard, with the Concordia College bookstore price-sticker still on it. For $6.95 I got both *Fear and Trembling* and *Repetition* translated by the Hongs. In their introduction they describe the way Kierkegaard invites us into a third way, a way intended by Aristotle to complement both theory (*theōria*) and practice (*praxis*) as ways of knowing, namely, poetics. Our epistemologies could benefit from more *poiēsis*, more poets of the possible; not only poets who write rhymes or verse, not only artists in metrical and metaphorical language, but as the Hongs describe Kierkegaard: "The poet is, then, as the word states, a maker, a maker in the realm of the possible rather than in the realm of what is or has been."[18]

Poets of the possible, leaning forward on tiptoes, drunk with hope for God's future, for what is being made new but going unperceived (Isa. 43:19), hypothesizing in concrete.[19] Peace-making poets of the possible, building bridges, as Paul Ricoeur proposes, "between the poetics of agape and the prose of justice, between the hymn and the formal rule."[20]

Many global traditions are finding their place within the Kente-like fabric of Western Christianity. They infuse our theoretically bound tradition with their poetical traditions, like dance and storytelling. These are gifts assuredly, serving to retranslate "the contents and effects of religious traditions"—but only to the ex-

18. Howard V. Hong and Edna H. Hong, "Historical Introduction," in Søren Kierkegaard, *Fear and Trembling/Repetition,* ed. and trans. Howard V. Hong and Edna H. Hong (Princeton: Princeton University Press, 1983), xxiii.

19. Hong and Hong, "Historical Introduction," xxv.

20. Paul Ricoeur, *The Course of Recognition,* trans. David Pellauer (Cambridge, MA: Harvard University Press, 2005), 224.

tent that we critique our hard, at times, frozen ontologies, and we engage the other as a divine-image bearer with humility and Holy Spirit–inspired hopefulness, confident always that God is greater. As I began, so I conclude with a word from Antje Jackelén: "In theology, Asian, African and Latin American voices have raised the consciousness that a *theologia absoluta et pura* cannot be the norm for doing theology. The norm must be a theology that can motivate and nourish hope."[21]

Narrative 2: Reimagining Race

Upon my arrival on the soil of the United States—I got here through a tunnel that joins Detroit and Windsor—I was processed at my own sort of Ellis Island. As a student beginning my new life at Concordia College in Ann Arbor, Michigan, I had to fill out the requisite campus census form. I knew most of the answers to this test—name, birthdate, and so forth—until I got to the category called Race/Ethnicity. There's a lot hidden in that slash, isn't there?

The first option was BLACK. I checked that box because my father is very black, Afro-Jamaican, and proud. The next box was WHITE. My mother is of Scottish Highland origin, tartan coat-of-arms and all. She is very white, almost see-through white, so I checked that box too. The next category was SPANISH-SURNAMED. That's where things began to get complicated. By Spanish-surnamed I think they meant then what such keepers of categories call Hispanic now. Funny how no one is really Hispanic until they arrive in the United States. Before that they're Panamanian or Paraguayan. They get here and we lump them. My last name

21. Antje Jackelén, "The Dynamics of Secularization, Atheism and the So-called Return of Religion and Its Significance for the Public Understanding of Science and Religion," in *Churrasco: A Theological Feast in Honor of Vítor Westhelle*, ed. Mary Philip, John Arthur Nunes, and Charles M. Collier (Eugene, OR: Pickwick, 2013), 24.

is spelled NUNES with an S, not a Z. It's actually Sephardic Jewish, but there was no such box on this form. Chased from Portugal five hundred years ago, these ancestors were nomadic and landed, my siblings and I liked to pretend as kids, as pirates of the Caribbean ("arrr," the international, trans-lingual pirate sound). Spain and Portugal border each other and the languages actually sounded very similar to me. I didn't speak either, but my surname was evidently one of them. Growing up in Canada, I spoke a bit of French, but there was no Francophone box. France and Spain also border each other. So, I reasoned, that's about four good reasons to check the Spanish-surnamed box, which dutifully I did.

After skipping the Asian/Pacific Islander box—which I was tempted to check because one never knows; these nomadic Nuneses very well could have floated Kon-Tiki–like out there—I finally came to International Student. Born in Montego Bay to a Canadian mother and a Jamaican father qualified me to check that box multiple times. My identity now fluidly established, I handed my check-heavy form to a tidy man, a quite fastidious and meticulous bow-tie-wearing man, the school census manager. I wouldn't say he was horrified, but there was this grimace and this mumbling, something about: "My data! You're skewing my data!" He and whoever prepared this form didn't think my hybridity was cool. This was long before we hybrids had a car named after us (ha!), and before we had a president who came from our race/ethnicity/tribe/people group requiring reimagination.

"Would you mind choosing just one?" the officious school official requested in a polite, evangelical tone. That day a new me was born, just like the Ellis Islanders who got their simplified, Anglicized names upon their arrival in New York's harbor. Like African slaves who were given the British names of their masters—Jackson, Jones, Johnson—that day I became something I hadn't been: black. Becoming African American awaited me by a decade.

First job for this new black person—that was before they, or should I say "we," were called African Americans—was to stir up a ruckus on this monochromatic Lutheran campus by creating a Black Students Organization and demanding our rights, specifically the right to celebrate Martin Luther King Jr. before his legacy became a holiday. We should also have included the demand for new census forms.

I like this story because it highlights, albeit with a little bit of late adolescent insolence, a lot of prophetic truth. The insight that people can't be boxed in predictable categories, and the foresight that the time will come when such arbitrary, silly categorizations are more the exception than the norm. The insight that there is one race and it's called human and like an insightful prophet named Martin Luther King Jr. said, with foresight, fifty years ago, "if we don't learn to live together as sisters and brothers, we will surely perish together as fools." I expect people of faith to know this better than most. The self-evident insight that all people are created with divine dignity in the eyes of their Creator, with as much diversity within so-called races as between them, and the foresight that the day will come when humans will, even if they disestablish race, find new senseless categories to define and exclude one another unless we speak the truth with love now.

Afterword

Today, Christianity is the world's largest religion, and two-thirds of the world's Christians live in Africa, Asia, and Latin America. As the center of Christianity has shifted from the global North to the global South, scholars have examined colonial missions that gave rise to these Christian communities, their postcolonial legacies, and emergent Christian theologies and rituals.[1] A prominent theme in this literature is that religious beliefs and practices are ultimately contextual, arising from specific historical circumstances, geographic locations, and encounters between religious (or non-religious) peoples. Alberto García and John Nunes's book *Wittenberg Meets the World: Reimagining the Reformation at the Margins* is situated within this scholarship by exploring the postcolonial

---

1. Philip Jenkins, *The Next Christendom: The Coming of Global Christianity* (New York: Oxford University Press, 2002); Lamin Sanneh and Joel A. Carpenter, eds., *The Changing Face of Christianity: Africa, the West, and the World* (New York: Oxford University Press, 2005); Dana Lee Robert, ed., *Converting Colonialism: Visions and Realities in Mission History, 1706–1914* (Grand Rapids: Eerdmans, 2008); Heather Sharkey, ed., *Cultural Conversions: Unexpected Consequences of Christian Missionary Encounters in the Middle East, Africa, and South Asia* (Syracuse, NY: Syracuse University Press, 2013); Melanie E. Trexler, *Evangelizing Lebanon: Baptists, Missions, and the Questions of Cultures* (Waco, TX: Baylor University Press, 2016).

legacy of Christianity, particularly Lutheranism, from the "margins," a term the authors use to characterize the global South and overlooked Christian communities in the US diaspora. García and Nunes challenge readers to think critically about the contexts in which the majority of Lutherans are established, where postcolonial legacies, poverty, political corruption, and violence are the norm. More specifically, García and Nunes challenge readers to consider what Lutherans from Africa and Latin America (and the excluded US diaspora) might teach those in the global North about the Reformation principle of justification as understood in terms of *martyria* (witness), *diakonia* (service), and *koinōnia* (fellowship).

The first challenge is centered on *martyria*, the witness about the good news of Christ that the church proclaims to the world. As Nunes reveals to readers, Southern Christians question the ways in which the church contributes to systems of sin that prohibit all people from fully experiencing God's mercy. These questions call Northern Christians to account for the idols they have created that undermine the worship of God, oppress God's children, and contribute to binary thinking of "us" and "them," "friend" and "enemy." Christians from the margins challenge these binaries, bearing witness to the good news that God's mercy is wide enough for all of humanity. But, for everyone to experience this divine gift, churches in the global North must unmask their sin and confront the context of exclusion operative in their churches and societies. Christians must recognize that the gospel the church bears witness to is not equally available to everyone when hierarchies of oppression or the valuation of one people group above another is present.

Unmasking sin is uncomfortable. People at the margins are asking Northern Christians to confront the reality of violence, poverty, and degradation that two-thirds of the global population experience daily, as well as the reality that people who are created in God's image are not treated as such. García warns readers that the call to unmask sin, particularly the sin of idolatry, is risky. Idolatry causes Northern Christians to think their actions and norms are rooted in Scripture;

painful is the charge to rethink the structures of power Northern Christians created and from which they benefit. Yet, if Northern Christians can listen to and learn from Christians from the margins, they will hear the invitation to proclaim the incarnate love of God. They will expand their notion of sin beyond that of the individual to a concept of sin as systemic. They will understand that the way to actualize God's mercy fully is to act on their love for their neighbors by dismantling the systems that humiliate, oppress, and undermine. As Nunes reminds readers, the creative disruption Christians from the margins offer enables the truths of Scripture to emerge anew, and encourages Christians from around the world to participate in *martyria* together with a passion to bear witness to the God of mercy who offers justification to all.

The second challenge García and Nunes present hinges on *diakonia*. Traditionally, Christians have understood *diakonia* as service *to* others, which is manifest in mission trips, clothing drives, and special offerings. Christians at the margins, however, challenge Northern Christians to reimagine what service means. As García describes, in the United States, immigrants, or those labeled "non-American" by the larger society, find themselves ghettoized in ethnic or ESL ministries, the recipients of short-term projects, and worshiping off-hours in the basements of church buildings. Given this context, Christians at the margins ask Northern churches to scrutinize their ministries: are churches acting sinfully by pursuing personal interests through ministries that are intent on increasing membership, or are churches acting saintly by pursuing community *with* and service *alongside* those at the margins?

The question is painful. It challenges churches to dissect ministries that have operated for decades and were designed with the intent to help people. Through assessments, distressing truths will be uncovered if churches realize their outreach did not have its desired effect and that their best intentions were overwhelmingly paternalistic. Churches and individuals will be convicted of their sin, viewing beloved ministries in a new light that might bring embarrassment and shame. Yet, if churches willingly undergo this critical assessment, Christians can learn what *diakonia* might look like if reimagined as service *with* the neighbor, not service *for* the neighbor. Nunes urges readers to understand that *diakonia* requires living, learning, and worshiping alongside and in partnership with those whom societies exclude. This re-envisioned *diakonia* requires Northern churches to ask and listen to what marginalized communities need, and together with these communities, reimagine incarnational ministries that empower neighbors to be present with each other in meaningful ways. Such a concept of *diakonia* compels Northern Christians to get out of their churches and into the streets to experience life with the marginalized. In the process, García and Nunes assure readers that Christians can live out the life of service to which they are called by God, and in mutual partnership can seek to overturn the systems that seek to snuff out full human flourishing.

The third, and perhaps most difficult, challenge is rooted in *koinōnia*. Most Christians around the world recognize the value of fellowship in community and its importance for bearing faithful witness to the gospel. However, Nunes reveals that those at the margins challenge all Christians to reimagine community as one in diversity. Specifically, Northern Christians are invited to reimagine a Christian community in which the majority are from the postcolonial global South or excluded diaspora, identify as persons of color, are women, and are poor. This community looks vastly different from the largely white, middle-class Lutheran congregations in the global North. Christians at the margins hold different interpretations of shared religious doctrines and practice their religious convictions in rituals unfamiliar to Christians in the global North. Northern Christians are summoned to embrace this diversity by demonstrating solidarity with those who are different, not because they are different or "other," but, as Nunes argues, because they are fellow human beings created in God's image, worthy of dignity and respect.

Such a challenge is unnerving for Christians in the global North. The risk of *koinōnia* could mean putting their bodies in the very places that marginalized Christians find themselves, including in front of police officers, armies, and other authorities. The risk of community could also mean speaking out vocally against systems of sin, including degrading political policies, corrupt politicians, and school curriculums that perpetuate exclusion and marginalization. Northern Christians will come to question their privilege, why they think the ways that they do, and how they treat others as a result. Participation in this kind of *koinōnia* can be uncomfortable. However, as García emphasizes, by contributing actively to a community in diversity, Northern Christians can learn what it truly means to be members of the body of Christ and to experience the Eucharist as a community. With those at the margins, they can reimagine what the kingdom of God might look like by celebrating their life *together* in the here-and-now and hoping for the kingdom to come.

Through their work, García and Nunes expose the need for more Lutherans in the global South and excluded diaspora to pen their own theologies, just as Gudina Tumsa and Leopoldo Sánchez have done.[2] They also demonstrate the need for scholars to conduct ethnographic studies and gather oral histories of congregations in order to learn more about what Lutherans believe and practice, identify the issues and theological doctrines that matter most to their communities, and give voice to the messages that these congregations want to share with their co-religionists. Hearing from these congregations gives us a new picture of the Reformation and its influence in the world. Yet, the challenge García and Nunes present still remains. In the twenty-first century, will those Christians living in the global North risk the status quo to reimagine the Reformation alongside Christians at the margins? Or will Christians

2. Gudina Tumsa, *Witness and Discipleship: Leadership of the Church in Multi-Ethnic Ethiopia in a Time of Revolution* (Addis Ababa: Gudina Tumsa Foundation, 2003), and Leopoldo A. Sánchez, *Teología de la santificación: la espiritualidad del cristiano* (St. Louis: Concordia, 2013).

continue to envision Lutheranism as predominantly planted in the global North, and overlook those in the global South and excluded diaspora who are imagining and experiencing the Reformation anew?

MELANIE TREXLER
Assistant Professor of Theology
(Islam and Muslim-Christian Relations)
Valparaiso University

For Discussion and Reflection

We hope that this book will be used in universities, seminaries, Bible institutes, and churches for dialogue and reflection. Toward this goal we offer the study questions below.

Preface

1. The authors' framework for theologizing is dually situated in an evangelical catholic tradition and a postcolonial critique.
   — What do the authors identify as an "evangelical catholic tradition" and as a "post-colonial critique"?
   — How do the authors employ these two dimensions in the book?
   — How do they apply this interrelationship in the art of theologizing in the twenty-first century?
   — Critique this approach. Do you find this approach useful or not in addressing postcolonialism?
   — Do you have other suggestions for offering a postcolonial critique?
2. In modernism the universal truth of reason takes priority and

in postmodernism the particularity of the human experience takes priority.

— How do the authors address these two uses of reason in their work?

— Note their preference for using the formula "I am where I think" rather than the Cartesian dictum, "I think, therefore I am." How do they take into consideration in this approach Luther's critique and use of reason?

— What do you propose as a salutary use or rejection of reason in theological discourse? Discuss this in light of the authors' proposal.

— How do Luther and the authors apply the Reformation principle of *solus Christus* (through Christ alone)? Do you agree or disagree with their application of this Reformation principle? Explain why. In your response make reference to the place and function of the incarnation in applying the *solus Christus* principle. How do the authors go beyond Luther's application of the *solus Christus* in affirmation of the incarnation from the margins? Do you find the principle of *solus Christus* useful for a Christian hermeneutics? Are there any weaknesses or limitations? Do you have some constructive criticisms to make concerning this approach?

3. The authors' point of departure is a borderland experience. Another word used by the authors is "diaspora." Chapter 1 defines and explains more precisely this point of departure.

— What is this point of departure?

— Do you find this approach useful in the study of theology and the Reformation?

— Is this approach disruptive in the way you do theology?

— If you have engaged in the art of theology from a mainstream North American perspective, how fair or unfair are the authors in their approach?

— What do you propose that needs to be re-evaluated or addressed? How do you propose to do this?

— Do you consider yourself a child of a diaspora? If so, what are some of the themes from the margins that need to be addressed that you believe the authors have neglected? How should those neglected themes be addressed?

Chapters 1 and 2

1. These chapters concentrate on the teaching of justification by faith from the margins.

   — How do perspectives regarding justification by grace, gained from non-English and non-Western settings, impact the way you view this doctrine on which the church stands or falls?

   — Why do the authors consider justification by faith a central point of departure in theologizing from the margins?

   — What important themes and perspectives are underscored by the authors as they reimagine the Reformation teaching of justification from the margins?

   — Why is the theme of the "God of life" a much-needed perspective for reimagining the "God of our justification" in the twenty-first century?

   — What is accentuated in chapter 1 under the theme of the "God of life" from the margins that has been generally missed by theologians doing theology from a European or North American perspective?

   — How do the themes of popular religiosity and eco-justice contribute to our understanding of the God of our justification as the God of life? Give some examples.

2. Chapter 1 describes the different meanings and applications for the teaching of justification in the sixteenth century.

   — Why do the authors prefer to speak of justification as commutative rather than retributive? How does this play out in reading justification by faith in Spanish?

— Do you believe that the theme of justice belongs within the realm of justification by faith? Should we employ this approach for addressing systemic and ecological sins beyond personal sins?

— Give reasons why you agree or disagree with the authors' proposal. How does your proposal in addressing these themes affect your Christian life and/or pastoral practice?

— Why do the authors stress that our understanding of God's righteousness must be reimagined in light of the action of the Holy Spirit? Reflect on this point in light of the Gospels.

— How do we apply here the principle of "Christ alone" (*solus Christus*) in light of Jesus's Galilean experience? How does this consideration affect our relationships in community and society? Identify examples and ways that this point of departure might be employed in pastoral ministry.

— How do the authors read the Sermon on the Mount from the perspective of the God of life? How does this reading enlighten the teaching of God's righteousness in Matthew? Discuss how this point of departure may be beneficial for pastoral ministry.

Chapters 3 and 4

1. These chapters are reflections on how to give witness to the gospel in light of the present atmosphere of exclusion in the world. They draw on the witness of the Reformation gospel from the margins.

— In what sense does our access to opportunity, privilege, and resources shift or diminish our notions of what it means to be a witness to Jesus Christ?

— How does chapter 3 focus on the meaning of a gracious God for our times? What first step is suggested to engage in this reimagining of God's grace for our times? Discuss this in light of Luther's lectures on the Minor Prophets. Comment on how helpful or hurtful the affirmation of American civil religion is for our witness of the gospel in the twenty-first century.

2. The Reformation identity has been shaped under four principles: *sola gratia, sola fides, sola scriptura, solus Christus*. Chapter 3 suggests adding one more *sola* in light of Luther's reading of the Gospel of John.

   — How does this focus help or hinder the reimagination of the gospel for our times?

   — How does Jesus's teaching in Matthew 5:38–41 help in our reimagination of the witness of the gospel? How does Wink's re-reading of this text help us to clarify Luther's commentary on this text? How does it help in offering an incarnational witness of Christ's love?

Chapters 5 and 6

1. Luther's 95 Theses express more than a critique of indulgences.

   — How do these theses express a resolution to love and serve our neighbor?

   — What theological themes does Luther use to encourage the church to practice a way of service? What does this service entail? Is it only a service of person to person, or does it also include the service of the church to a community?

2. *Diakonia*, service to the world grounded in a gospel of love, is central to the Lutheran identity and to Luther's teaching. This is poignantly stated by Luther in his treatise *The Freedom of the Christian* (1520). There Luther states: "A Christian is a perfectly free lord of all, subject to none. A Christian is a perfectly dutiful servant of all, subject to all . . . and [Paul says] in Rom. 13:8 'Owe no one anything except to love one another'" (*LW* 31:244).

   — Discuss how Luther's teaching on *diakonia* needs further

reimagination for our times and for a ministry from the margins. What are Luther's strengths and weaknesses in his affirmation of service to neighbor and world?

— What is the role of the Holy Spirit in our pursuit of a *diakonia* from the margins? What does this role mean for ministry in the twenty-first century?

— How does the Holy Spirit offer a creative disruption for a witness from the margins? How has this been expressed in Latino communities of faith? Offer specific examples from your own particular locus (place) in community.

3. The principle of the priesthood of all believers is essential for service in the world.

— How has this Reformation principle been neglected and misused by the heirs of the Reformation?

— How might this principle be reimagined for service within the margins? Discuss this in light of specific examples offered in these essays. Discuss this in light of your own community of faith.

Chapters 7 and 8

1. Life together (*koinōnia*) and service (*diakonia*) are important marks of the church.

— How do *koinōnia* and *diakonia* mutually reinforce each other in the day-to-day ministry of Christian communities?

2. North American Protestant and evangelical theologies have been marked by individualism. The personal meaning and salvation of the individual is primarily sought after. This way of thinking has also been part of the mindset of many Catholics and evangelical catholics in the United States.

— Discuss these trends and attitudes within North American church life. Do so in light of Luther, Paul, and recent Catholic communion ecclesiology. What needs to be refocused for building a *koinōnia* for our time and place in North America?

— How does a cruciform discipleship impact our life together (*koinōnia*) at the margins? How does this point of departure guide our teaching and application of spiritual gifts?

3. Most people envision exercising a life in *koinōnia* by helping their community of faith, friends, and family.

— Why is this not enough in creating a community of faith from the margins?

— Respond to the statement, "the kingdom of God must be redefined as the 'kin-dom' of God in pursuing a Latino ecclesiology."

— Why does the *koinōnia* of the justified need to move beyond serving the physical needs of the poor and needy? How does this *koinōnia* need to address the issue of human identity?

— How do we need to refocus our speech and witness concerning human identity within Latino communities? How do fiestas within Latino communities contribute to this discussion? What needs to be reimagined to ground fiestas in a festive hope?

— How important is the horizon of apocalyptic hope for constructing a living *koinōnia* from the margins? How has this perspective been abused and misused in Christian witness and worship? How can we correct these abuses? How might we be empowered to live a life of festive hope within the margins?

Works Cited

Alfaro, Sammy. *Divino Compañero: Toward a Hispanic Pentecostal Christology*. Princeton Theological Monograph Series. Eugene, OR: Wipf and Stock, 2010.

Álvarez, Eliseo Pérez. "In Memory of Me: A Hispanic/Latino Christology beyond Borders." In *Teología en Conjunto: A Collaborative Hispanic Protestant Theology*, edited by José Rodríguez and Loida I. Martell-Otero, 33–49. Louisville: Westminster John Knox, 1997.

Aponte, Edwin David, and Miguel A. De La Torre, eds. *Handbook of Latina/o Theologies*. St. Louis: Chalice, 2006.

Atkinson, James. *Martin Luther and the Birth of Protestantism*. Atlanta: John Knox, 1968.

Barnett, Michael N. *Empire of Humanity: A History of Humanitarianism*. Ithaca, NY: Cornell University Press, 2011.

Bayer, Oswald. *Martin Luther's Theology: A Contemporary Interpretation*. Translated by Thomas H. Trapp. Grand Rapids: Eerdmans, 2007.

Bellini, Peter. "The Processio-Missio Connection: A Starting Point in Missio Trinitatis or Overcoming the Immanent-Economic Divide in Missio Trinitatis." *Wesleyan Theological Journal* (October 2014).

Benavides, Luis E. "The Spirit." In *Handbook of Latina/o Theologies*, edited by Edwin David Aponte and Miguel A. De La Torre, 29–31. St. Louis: Chalice, 2006.

Bethge, Renate. *Dietrich Bonhoeffer: A Brief Life*. Minneapolis: Augsburg Fortress, 1991.

Boff, Leonardo. *Church, Charism and Power*. Translated by John W. Diercksmeier. New York: Crossroad, 1981.

————. *Iglesia: carisma y poder*. Santander: Sal Terrae, 1981.

Bonhoeffer, Dietrich. *Creation and Fall: A Theological Exposition of Genesis 1–3*, edited by John W. de Gruchy, translated by Douglas Stephen Bax. Dietrich Bonhoeffer Works 3. Minneapolis: Fortress, 1997.

————. *Life Together; Prayerbook of the Bible*. Edited by Geffrey B. Kelly, translated by Daniel W. Bloesch and James H. Burtness. Dietrich Bonhoeffer Works 5. Minneapolis: Fortress, 1996.

Braaten, Carl E. *That All May Believe: A Theology of the Gospel and the Mission of the Church*. Grand Rapids: Eerdmans, 2008.

Breen, Michael, and Sally Breen. *Family on Mission*. Pawleys Island: 3DM, 2014.

Caputo, John D. *What Would Jesus Deconstruct? The Good News of Postmodernism for the Church*. Grand Rapids: Baker Academic, 2007.

Chemnitz, Martin. *Loci Theologici*. Translated by J. A. O. Preus. St. Louis: Concordia, 1989.

Chesterton, G. K. *Heretics*. Rockville, MD: Serenity, 2009.

Coiran, E. M. *A Short History of Decay*. Translated by Richard Howard. London: Quartet Book, 1990.

Collins, John J. *The Apocalyptic Imagination: An Introduction to Jewish Apocalyptic Literature*. 2nd ed. Grand Rapids: Eerdmans, 1998.

Concilio Vaticano II. Declaraciones, Decretos. Madrid: Biblioteca de Autores Cristianos, 1970.

Cullmann, Oscar. *The Christology of the New Testament*. Philadelphia: Westminster, 1963.

Davies, W. D., and Dale C. Allison Jr. *A Critical and Exegetical Commentary on the Gospel according to Saint Matthew*. Edinburgh: T&T Clark, 1988–97.

Deck, Allan Figueroa. *Francis, Bishop of Rome*. Mahwah, NJ: Paulist, 2016.

De La Torre, Miguel. *Doing Christian Ethics from the Margins*. Maryknoll, NY: Orbis, 2004.

Díaz, Miguel. "Outside the Survival of Community There Is No Salvation: A U.S. Hispanic Catholic Contribution to Soteriology." In *Building Bridges, Doing Justice: Constructing a Latino/a Ecumenical Theology*, edited by Orlando E. Espín. Maryknoll, NY: Orbis, 2009.

Die Bekenntnis Schriften. Göttingen: Vandenhoeck & Ruprecht, 1979.

Dieter, Theodore. "Why Does Luther's Doctrine of Justification Matter Today?" In *The Global Luther: A Theologian for Modern Times*, edited by Christine Helmer. Minneapolis: Fortress, 2009.

Dussel, Enrique. *The Invention of the Americas*. Translated by Michael D. Barber. New York: Continuum, 1995.

Eide, Oeyvind, ed. *Revolution and Religion in Ethiopia: The Growth and Persecution of the Mekane Yesus Church, 1974–85*. Oxford: J. Currey, 2000.

Elizondo, Virgilio. *The Future Is Mestizo: Life Where Cultures Meet*. Boulder: University Press of Colorado, 2000.

———. *Galilean Journey: The Mexican-American Promise*. Maryknoll, NY: Orbis, 1983.

———. "Mestizaje as a Locus of Theological Reflection." In *Beyond Borders: Writings of Virgilio Elizondo and Friends*, edited by Timothy Matovina. Maryknoll, NY: Orbis, 2000.

Erevia, Angela. *Quinceañera*. San Antonio, TX: Mexican American Center, 1980.

Espín, Orlando E. "500 Years after the Posting of Luther's Theses: A Catholic Perspective." In *Our Ninety-Five Theses: Five Hundred Years after the Reformation*, edited by Alberto L. García and Justo L. González. Orlando: Asociación para La Educatión Teológica Hispana, 2016.

———. *Idol and Grace: On Traditioning and Subversive Hope*. Maryknoll, NY: Orbis, 2014.

———, ed. *Building Bridges, Doing Justice: Constructing a Latino/a Ecumenical Theology*. Maryknoll, NY: Orbis, 2009.

———, and Miguel H. Díaz, eds. *From the Heart of Our People: Latino/a Explorations of Catholic Systematic Theology*. Maryknoll, NY: Orbis, 1999.

García, Alberto L. "Leonardo Boff." In *The Encyclopedia of Christian Civilization*, edited by George Thomas Kurian, 1:287–90. 4 vols. Sussex: Wiley-Blackwell, 2012.

———. "Signposts for Global Witness in Luther's Theology of the Cross." In *The Theology of the Cross for the 21st Century*, edited by Alberto L. García and A. R. Victor Raj. St. Louis: Concordia, 2002.

———. "Theology of the Cross: A Critical Study of Leonardo Boff's and Jon Sobrino's Theology of the Cross in Light of Luther's Theology of the Cross as Interpreted by Luther Scholars." PhD diss., Lutheran School of Theology at Chicago, 1987.

————, and Rubén D. Domínguez. *Introducción a la vida y teología de Martín Lutero*. Nashville: Abingdon, 2008.

————, and Justo L. González, eds. *Our Ninety-Five Theses: Five Hundred Years after the Reformation*. Asociación para La Educatión Teológica Hispana, 2016.

————, and A. R. Victor Raj, eds. *The Theology of the Cross for the 21st Century*. St. Louis: Concordia, 2002.

————, and Susan K. Wood, eds. *Critical Issues in Ecclesiology: Essays in Honor of Carl E. Braaten*. Edited by Alberto L. García and Susan K. Wood. Grand Rapids: Eerdmans, 2011.

García-Villoslada, Ricardo. *Martín Lutero*. Vols. 1 and 2. Madrid: Biblioteca de Autores Cristianos, 1973.

Gibbs, Jeffrey A. *Concordia Commentary on Matthew 1:1–11:1*. St. Louis: Concordia, 2004.

Goizueta, Roberto S. *Caminemos con Jesús: Toward a Hispanic/Latino Theology of Accompaniment*. Maryknoll, NY: Orbis, 1995.

————. "Fiesta: Life in the Subjunctive." In *From the Heart of Our People: Latino/a Explorations of Catholic Systematic Theology*, edited by Orlando O. Espín and Miguel H. Díaz. Maryknoll, NY: Orbis, 1999.

González, Justo L. *Acts: The Gospel of the Spirit*. Maryknoll, NY: Orbis, 2001.

————. *Faith and Wealth: A History of Early Christian Ideas on the Origin, Significance, and Use of Money*. Eugene, OR: Wipf and Stock, 2002.

————. "In Quest of a Protestant Hispanic Ecclesiology." In *Teología en Conjunto: A Collaborative Hispanic Protestant Theology*, edited by José David Rodríguez and Loida I. Martell-Otero. Louisville: Westminster John Knox, 1997.

González, Michelle A. "Is Pope Francis the First Latin American Pope? The Politics of Identity in America." In *Pope Francis in Postcolonial Reality*, edited by Nicolas Panotto. Borderless, 2015.

Gritsch, Eric W. *Reformer without a Church: The Life and Thought of Thomas Muentzer (1488?–1525)*. Philadelphia: Fortress, 1967.

Gutiérrez, Gustavo. *The God of Life*. Translated by Matthew J. O'Connell. Maryknoll, NY: Orbis, 1991.

Hackmann, E. Edward. "Augustine and the Concept of Person." *Lutheran Theological Review* 3, no. 2 (Spring–Summer 1991).

Hall, Basil. "*Hoc est corpus meum*: The Centrality of the Real Presence for

Luther." In *Luther: Theologian for Catholics and Protestants*, edited by George Hule. Edinburgh: T&T Clark, 1985.

Helmer, Christine, ed. *The Global Luther: A Theologian for Modern Times*. Minneapolis: Fortress, 2009.

Hinlicky, Paul R. *Luther and the Beloved Community: A Path for Christian Theology after Christendom*. Grand Rapids: Eerdmans, 2010.

Hule, George, ed. *Luther: Theologian for Catholics and Protestants*. Edinburgh: T&T Clark, 1985.

Huntington, Samuel P. *Who Are We? The Challenges to America's National Identity*. New York: Simon and Schuster, 2004.

Husbands, Mark, and Daniel J. Treier, eds. *Justification: What's at Stake in the Current Debates*. Downers Grove, IL: InterVarsity, 2004.

Isasi-Díaz, Ada María. *La Lucha Continues: Mujerista Theology*. Maryknoll, NY: Orbis, 2004.

———, and Fernando Segovia, eds. *Hispanic/Latino Theology*. Minneapolis: Fortress, 2000.

Jackelén, Antje. "The Dynamics of Secularization, Atheism and the So-called Return of Religion and Its Significance for the Public Understanding of Science and Religion." In *Churrasco: A Theological Feast in Honor of Vítor Westhelle*, edited by Mary Philip, John Arthur Nunes, and Charles M. Collier. Eugene, OR: Pickwick, 2013.

Jenkins, Philip. *The Next Christendom: The Coming of Global Christianity*. New York: Oxford University Press, 2002.

Joest, Wilfred. *Ontologie der Person bei Luther*. Göttingen: Vandenhoeck & Ruprecht, 1967.

Johnson, Elizabeth A. *Quest for the Living God: Mapping Frontiers in the Theology of God*. New York: Continuum, 2011.

Joint Declaration on the Doctrine of Justification by the Lutheran World Federation and Roman Catholic Church, 1999.

Juneja, Renu. *Caribbean Transactions: The Making of West Indian Culture in Literature*. London: Macmillan, 1996.

Just, Arthur A. *Concordia Commentary on Luke 9:51–24:53*. St. Louis: Concordia, 1997.

Kierkegaard, Søren. *Fear and Trembling/Repetition*. Edited and translated by Howard V. Hong and Edna H. Hong. Princeton: Princeton University Press, 1983.

King, Martin Luther, Jr., and James Melvin Washington. *A Testament of*

Hope: The Essential Writings and Speeches of Martin Luther King Jr. San Francisco: HarperSanFrancisco, 1991.

Kittelson, James. *Luther the Reformer: The Story of the Man and His Career.* Minneapolis: Fortress, 1986.

Kolb, Robert. "Contemporary Lutheran Understanding of the Doctrine of Justification." In *Justification: What's at Stake in the Current Debates,* edited by Mark Husbands and Daniel J. Treier. Downers Grove, IL: InterVarsity, 2004.

———, and Timothy J. Wengert, eds. *The Book of Concord.* Minneapolis: Fortress, 2000.

———, Irene Dingel, and L'Ubomír Batka, eds. *The Oxford Handbook of Martin Luther's Theology.* Oxford: Oxford University Press, 2014.

Ladaria, Luis F. *The Living and True God: The Mystery of the Trinity.* Translated and revised by María Isabel Reyna and Liam Kelly. Miami: Convivium, 2010.

León-Portilla, Miguel. *Tonatzín Guadalupe: Pensamiento náhuatl y pensamiento cristiano en el "Nicanmopohua."* México, D.F.: Fondo de Cultura Económica, 2000.

Lienhard, Marc. *Luther: Witness to Jesus Christ.* Translated by Edwin H. Robertson. Minneapolis: Augsburg, 1982.

Lindberg, Carter. *Beyond Charity: Reformation Initiatives for the Poor.* Minneapolis: Fortress, 1993.

Lortz, Joseph. "The Basic Elements of Luther's Intellectual Life." In *Catholic Scholars Dialogue with Luther,* edited by Jared Wicks. Chicago: Loyola University Press, 1972.

Louw, J. P., and Eugene A. Nida, eds. *Greek-English Lexicon of the New Testament: Based on Semantic Domains.* 2nd ed. New York: United Bible Societies, 1996.

Luna, Anita de. "Popular Religion and Spirituality." In *Handbook of Latina/o Theologies,* edited by Edwin David Aponte and Miguel A. De La Torre. St. Louis: Chalice, 2006.

Luther, Martin. *D. Martin Luthers Werke: Kritische Gesamtausgabe.* 58 vols. Weimar: Herman Böhlaus, 1833–1999.

———. *Early Theological Writings.* Translated and edited by James Atkinson. Philadelphia: Westminster, 1955–76.

———. *Luther's Works American Edition.* Edited by Jaroslav Pelikan and Helmut T. Lehman (vols. 1–55) and Christopher Boyd Brown (vols.

56–75). St. Louis: Concordia; Philadelphia: Muhlenberg and Fortress, 1955–86; 2007–.

———. *Select Works of Martin Luther*. Translated by Henry Cole. 4 vols. London: T. Bensley, 1924–26.

Lutheran Service Book. St. Louis: Concordia, 2006.

Lutheran World Federation and the Pontifical Council for Promoting Christian Unity. *From Conflict to Communion: Lutheran-Catholic Common Commemoration of the Reformation in 2017*. Leipzig: Evangelische Verlagsanstalt, 2013.

Mangina, Joseph L. "The Cross-Shaped Church: A Pauline Amendment to the Ecclesiology of Koinonia." In *Critical Issues in Ecclesiology*, edited by Alberto L. García and Susan K. Wood. Grand Rapids: Eerdmans, 2011.

Mannermaa, Tuomo. *Two Kinds of Love: Martin's Luther's Religious World*. Translated and edited by Kirsi I. Stjerna. Minneapolis: Fortress, 2010.

Matovina, Timothy, ed. *Beyond Borders: Writings of Virgilio Elizondo and Friends*. Maryknoll, NY: Orbis, 2000.

Mattes, Mark. "Luther on Justification as Forensic and Effective." In *The Oxford Handbook of Martin Luther's Theology*, edited by Robert Kolb, Irene Dingel, and L'Ubomír Batka. Oxford: Oxford University Press, 2014.

McGrath, Alister E. *Iustitia Dei: A History of the Christian Doctrine of Justification*. Vols. 1 and 2. Cambridge: Cambridge University Press, 1986.

Meeks, Wayne. *The Social World of the Apostle Paul*. New Haven: Yale University Press, 1983.

Méndez, P. Pedro Alarcón. *El Amor de Jesús vivo en la Virgen de Guadalupe*. Bloomington, IN: Palibrio, 2013.

Mignolo, Walter D. *Global Histories/Local Designs: Coloniality, Subaltern Knowledges, and Border Thinking*. Princeton: Princeton University Press, 2012.

Nanko-Fernández, Carmen. *Theologizing in Espanglish*. Maryknoll, NY: Orbis, 2010.

Omolo, Tom Joseph. "Luther in Africa." In *The Oxford Handbook of Martin Luther's Theology*, edited by Robert Kolb, Irene Dingel, and L'Ubomír Batka. Oxford: Oxford University Press, 2014.

Pannenberg, Wolfhart. *Systematic Theology*. Vol. 3. Grand Rapids: Eerdmans, 1998.

Panotto, Nicolas, ed. *Pope Francis in Postcolonial Reality*. Borderless, 2015.

Pelikan, Jaroslav. *The Christian Tradition: A History of the Development of Doctrine.* Vol. 4. Chicago: University of Chicago Press, 1984.

———. *The Riddle of Roman Catholicism: Its History, Its Beliefs, Its Future.* London: Hodder and Stoughton, 1960.

———. *The Vindication of Tradition.* New Haven: Yale University Press, 1984.

Peterson, Cheryl M. "Lutheran Principles for Ecclesiology." In *Critical Issues in Ecclesiology,* edited by Alberto L. García and Susan K. Wood. Grand Rapids: Eerdmans, 2011.

Philip, Mary, John Arthur Nunes, and Charles M. Collier, eds. *Churrasco: A Theological Feast in Honor of Vítor Westhelle.* Eugene, OR: Pickwick, 2013.

Polhill, John B. *The New American Commentary: Acts.* Nashville: Broadman and Holman, 1992.

Prenter, Regin. *Spiritus Creator.* Translated by John M. Jensen. Philadelphia: Muhlenberg, 1953.

Recinos, Harold. "The Barrio as a Locus of a New Church." In *Hispanic/Latino Theology,* edited by Ada María Isasi-Diaz and Fernando Segovia. Minneapolis: Fortress, 2000.

Ricoeur, Paul. *The Course of Recognition.* Translated by David Pellauer. Cambridge, MA: Harvard University Press, 2005.

Riebe-Estrella, Gary. "Pueblo and Church." In *From the Heart of Our People: Latino/a Explorations of Catholic Systematic Theology,* edited by Orlando O. Espín and Miguel H. Díaz. Maryknoll, NY: Orbis, 1999.

Rivera-Pagán, Luis N. *Essays from the Margins.* Eugene, OR: Cascade, 2014.

Robert, Dana Lee, ed. *Converting Colonialism: Visions and Realities in Mission History, 1706–1914.* Grand Rapids: Eerdmans, 2008.

Rodriguez, Daniel A. *A Future for the Latino Church: Witness for Multilingual, Multigenerational Hispanic Congregations.* Downers Grove, IL: InterVarsity, 2011.

Rodriguéz, Isaías A. "A Reflection Concerning Anglicanism and the Hispanic World." In *Our Ninety-Five Theses: Five Hundred Years after the Reformation,* edited by Alberto L. García and Justo L. González. Orlando: Asociación para La Educación Teológica Hispana, 2016.

Rodríguez, Jeanette. *Our Lady of Guadalupe.* Austin: University of Texas Press, 2005.

———. *Stories We Live (Cuentos Que Vivimos): Hispanic Women's Spirituality.* New York: Paulist, 1996.

Rodríguez, José, and Loida I. Martell-Otero, eds. *Teología en Conjunto: A Collaborative Hispanic Protestant Theology*. Louisville: Westminster John Knox, 1997.

Rosen, Michael. *Dignity: Its History and Meaning*. Cambridge, MA: Harvard University Press, 2012.

Ruiz, Jean-Pierre. *Reading from the Edges: The Bible and People on the Move*. Maryknoll, NY: Orbis, 2011.

———. "The Word Became Flesh and the Flesh Becomes Word: Notes toward a U.S. Latino/a Theology." In *Building Bridges, Doing Justice: Constructing a Latino/a Ecumenical Theology*, edited by Orlando E. Espín. Maryknoll, NY: Orbis, 2009.

Sacks, Jonathan. "Nostalgia for the Numinous" (a review of *Terry Eagleton's Culture and the Death of God*). *Jewish Review of Books* 18 (Summer 2014).

Sánchez, Leopoldo A. *Teología de la santificación: la espiritualidad del cristiano*. St. Louis: Concordia, 2013.

Sanneh, Lamin. *Religion and the Variety of Culture*. Valley Forge, PA: Trinity, 1996.

———, and Joel A. Carpenter, eds. *The Changing Face of Christianity: Africa, the West, and the World*. New York: Oxford University Press, 2005.

Sasse, Herman. *We Confess the Sacraments*. Translated by Norman Nagel. St. Louis: Concordia, 1985.

Scaer, David P. *Discourses in Matthew: Jesus Teaches the Church*. St. Louis: Concordia, 2004.

Schlink, Edmund. *Theology of the Lutheran Confessions*. Translated by P. Koehneke and J. A. Bownan. Philadelphia: Fortress, 1961.

Schwambach, Claus. *Rechtfertigungsgeschehen und Befreiungs prozess: Die Eschatologien von Martin Luther und Leonardo Boff im kritischen Gespräch*. Göttingen: Vandenhoeck & Ruprecht, 2004.

Schwanke, Johannes. "Luther's Theology of Creation." In *The Oxford Handbook of Martin Luther's Theology*, edited by Robert Kolb, Irene Dingel, and L'Ubomír Batka. Oxford: Oxford University Press, 2014.

Sharkey, Heather, ed. *Cultural Conversions: Unexpected Consequences of Christian Missionary Encounters in the Middle East, Africa, and South Asia*. Syracuse, NY: Syracuse University Press, 2013.

Sider, Robert D. *Christian and Pagan in the Roman Empire: The Witness of Tertullian.* Washington, DC: Catholic University of America Press, 2001.

Sittler, Joseph. *The Ecology of Faith.* Philadelphia: Muhlenberg, 1961.

Sobrino, Jon. *Archbishop Romero: Memories and Reflection.* Maryknoll, NY: Orbis, 1990.

Solberg, Mary M. *Compelling: A Feminist Proposal for an Epistemology of the Cross.* New York: State University of New York Press, 1997.

Solivan, Samuel. "Sources of a Hispanic/Latino American Theology: A Pentecostal Perspective." In *Hispanic/Latino Theology*, edited by Ada María Isasi-Diaz and Fernando Segovia. Minneapolis: Fortress, 2000.

———. *The Spirit, Pathos and Liberation: Toward an Hispanic Pentecostal Theology.* Sheffield: Sheffield Academic Press, 1998.

Strohl, Jane E. "Luther's Eschatology." In *The Oxford Handbook of Martin Luther's Theology*, edited by Robert Kolb, Irene Dingel, and Ĺ'Ubomír Batka. Oxford: Oxford University Press, 2014.

Taylor, Charles. *Sources of the Self.* Cambridge: Cambridge University Press, 1989.

Tertullian. *Ad Martyres.* In *The Ante-Nicene Fathers.* Vol. 3. Buffalo, NY: Christian Literature Company, 1895.

Theissen, Gerd. *The Social Setting of Pauline Christianity: Essays on Corinth.* Philadelphia: Fortress, 1982.

Thomas, Norman E. "Radical Mission in a Post-9/11 World: Creative Dissonances." *International Bulletin* (January 2005): 2–7.

Torrance, T. F. "The Eschatological Faith: Martin Luther." In *Luther: Theologian for Catholics and Protestants*, edited by George Hule. Edinburgh: T&T Clark, 1985.

Trexler, Melanie E. *Evangelizing Lebanon: Baptists, Missions, and the Questions of Cultures.* Waco, TX: Baylor University Press, 2016.

Tumsa, Gudina. "Memorandum to Ato Emmanuel Abraham, President, ECMY; from Gudina Tumsa, General Secretary, ECMY Re: Some Issues Requiring Discussions and Decisions." In *Revolution and Religion in Ethiopia: The Growth and Persecution of the Mekane Yesus Church, 1974–85.* Oxford: J. Currey, 2000.

———. "The Role of a Christian in a Given Society." In *Revolution and Religion in Ethiopia: The Growth and Persecution of the Mekane Yesus Church, 1974–85.* Oxford: J. Currey, 2000.

———. "Serving the Whole Man: A Responsible Church Ministry and Flexible International Aid Relationship." In *Proclamation and Human*

Development. LWF Documentation from a Lutheran World Federation Consultation in Nairobi, Kenya, October 21–25, 1974. Geneva: Lutheran World Federation, 1974.

———. *Witness and Discipleship: Leadership of the Church in Multi-Ethnic Ethiopia in a Time of Revolution.* Addis Ababa: Gudina Tumsa Foundation, 2000.

Villafañe, Eldín. *The Liberating Spirit: Toward an Hispanic American Pentecostal Social Ethic.* Grand Rapids: Eerdmans, 1993.

Volf, Miroslav. *Exclusion and Embrace: A Theological Exploration of Identity, Otherness, and Reconciliation.* Nashville: Abingdon, 1996.

Walcott, Derek. *Bounty.* New York: Farrar, Straus and Giroux, 1998.

———. *What the Twilight Says.* New York: Farrar, Straus and Giroux, 1998.

Westhelle, Vitor. *The Scandalous God: The Use and Abuse of the Cross.* Minneapolis: Fortress, 2009.

Wicks, Jared, ed. *Catholic Scholars Dialogue with Luther.* Chicago: Loyola University Press, 1972.

Wiesel, Elie. Acceptance speech. In *The Nobel Prizes 1986*, edited by Wilhelm Odelberg. Stockholm: Nobel Foundation, 1987.

Wingren, Gustaf. *Luther on Vocation.* Translated by Carl M. Rasmussen. Philadelphia: Muhlenberg, 1957.

Wink, Walter. *Jesus and Nonviolence: A Third Way.* Minneapolis: Fortress, 2003.

Young, Iris Marion, and Danielle S. Allen. *Justice and the Politics of Difference.* Princeton: Princeton University Press, 2011.

Index of Names

Index of Subjects

Amos, book of, Luther's commentary on, 52–54
Augustine, on justice, 29

Baptism, Luther on, 89
Borderland faith, 3–4

Church, definition of, 99
Civil religion: American identity in, 56–57; definition of, 56
Creation, doctrine of: and eco-justice, 35–36; and justice, 29; and redemption, 29; and sin structures, 33
Creative disruption: as a generational dynamic, 73–74; as interpretative principle, 70–71

Diakonia: in Acts 5, 97–100; definition of, 81; in Latino communities, 92–93; as mercy, 105–6; as vocation, 89–90; as the work of the Holy Spirit, 95–96
Diaspora: definition of, 5; as hermeneutical key, xvi, 3–5, 158; as unfinished identity, 6–7

Ecclesiology: ecclesial *koinōnia*, 118–19; and spiritual gifts, 119–29
Eco-justice, 32–33; and doctrine of creation, 35–36
Everyday life (*lo cotidiano*), the search for God in: definition and application, 2

Fides caritate formata: Luther and Aquinas on, 62
From Conflict to Communion: on *diakonia*, 80; on justification, 10–11

Grace, and *agapē* love, 60–62

Heidelberg Disputation (1518), 61–62, 81, 120–21
Holy Spirit: in *diakonia*, 110–11; in vocation, 88–90; work of in Acts, 3

Identity: existential vs. borderland, 5–6; the shaping of American vs. Latino, 56–57
Idolatry: definition of, 50; in Minor

Index of Scripture References

CPSIA information can be obtained
at www.ICGtesting.com
Printed in the USA
LVHW101810090422
715749LV00001B/12